FALSE CHOICES

FALSE CHOICES

*The Faux Feminism of
Hillary Rodham Clinton*

Edited by
Liza Featherstone

With contributions from
Medea Benjamin, Fred Block, Margaret Corvid,
Zillah Eisenstein, Belén Fernández, Laura Flanders,
Kathleen Geier, Frances Fox Piven, Amber A'Lee Frost,
Megan Erickson Kilpatrick, Catherine Liu,
Tressie McMillan Cottom, Donna Murch,
Yasmin Nair, Maureen Tkacik

VERSO
London • New York

First published by Verso 2016
The collection © Verso Books 2016
Contributions © The contributors 2016

1 3 5 7 9 10 8 6 4 2

Verso
UK: 6 Meard Street, London W1F 0EG
US: 20 Jay Street, Suite 1010, Brooklyn, NY 11201
versobooks.com

Verso is the imprint of New Left Books

ISBN-13: 978-1-78478-461-4 (PB)
ISBN-13: 978-1-78478-462-1 (US EBK)
ISBN-13: 978-1-78478-463-8 (UK EBK)

British Library Cataloguing in Publication Data
A catalogue record for this book is available from the British Library

Library of Congress Cataloging-in-Publication Data
A catalog record for this book is available from the Library of Congress

Typeset in Garamond Pro by MJ & N Gavan, Truro, Cornwall
Printed in the US by Maple Press

Contents

PROLOGUE

Clinton Contention

Laura Flanders

A play in one act.

CHARACTERS: *Laura and Elizabeth, a couple in their middle years.*
SETTING: *A New York City loft.*
TIME: *October 13, 2015, the first Democratic debate of the 2016 presidential election.*

ACT I

SCENE I

ELIZABETH

It's starting! Come on!

LAURA

Wait, while I bate my breath.

(On TV: ANDERSON COOPER: We are live at the Wynn Resort in Las Vegas for the CNN/Facebook Democratic Debate...)

LAURA

A casino! Perfect. A company that parts us from our money teamed up with one that parts us from our data. The presidential process, courtesy of gamblers and con men. How perfect! With advertising, I see, from Lockheed Martin.

ELIZABETH

Look. There she is. Doesn't she make you proud?

LAURA

As proud as Margaret Thatcher.

ELIZABETH

Oh come on.

LAURA

Eight years on, same couch, same candidate, same point of contention.

ELIZABETH

Hush. I'm trying to listen.

(On TV: Sen. LINCOLN CHAFEE: I've had no scandals...
Sen. JIM WEBB: I know where my loyalties are...
Gov. MARTIN O'MALLEY: I am very clear about my principles...)

ELIZABETH

Scandals, loyalties, principles… Do you think they're trying to get a dig in?

LAURA

Ya think? It's dog-whistle Hillary baiting, the Democratic version. The Dems can't go in for the Hillary Clinton nutcracker dolls or the sexist swipes at her ambition or her age, but if they can say the word "scandal" often enough, it'll trigger the same script. They clearly haven't noticed that attacks on her character only seem to make her stronger, at least among moderate women voters. Clinton's numbers rise in lockstep with feminist hackles. I hear the sound of pen on check even before she says a word.

ELIZABETH

Here she goes.

(On TV: HILLARY CLINTON: For me this is about bringing our country together again. And I will do everything to heal the divides – the divides economically because there's too much inequality; the racial divides; the continuing discrimination against the LGBT community—so that we work together and yes, finally fathers will be able to say to their daughters, you, too can grow up to be president.)

ELIZABETH

That's my girl! Heal the divides. LGBT! Bill was the first president even to say the word "gay." He made history and she'll make history. Just like she said. Forever, girls will grow up knowing they can be president. That's a game changer.

LAURA

Same old game. What's the liberal version of dog whistle? Catcall? Say the words race and inequality often enough; get your tongue around "LGBT" with the right initials in the right order, and your people will think you've said something significant. That's Democratic identity politics in action: win over your voting base identities while guaranteeing nothing on the politics.

And may I just say, it's not a disembodied "racial divide" that's killing Black Americans—it's white supremacy. Chattel slavery—*a racial divide?* Just what sort of "together again" country does she imagine bringing us back to?

ELIZABETH

Oh come on. Can you really deny that having our first female president would be historic?

LAURA

No, I can't. But an opportunity for one is a pretty meager antidote to the jobs crisis.

ELIZABETH

A female commander-in-chief?

LAURA

Why not murderer-in-chief? *Torturer-in-chief?* The service sector's crammed with women doing nasty, dirty, demeaning jobs. Maybe commander-in-chief—with its very peculiar requirement of power-lust plus pandering—is one bad public job we could leave to others.

ELIZABETH

You're being ridiculous.

*(On TV: COOPER: Just for the record, are you a progressive or are you
a moderate?*
*CLINTON: I'm a progressive but I'm a progressive who likes to get
things done. And I know how to find common ground and I know
how to stand my ground, and I have proved that every position
that I've had, even dealing with Republicans who never had a good
word to say about me, honestly, we found ways to work together…)*

LAURA

For the record? What's the good of a record if you're just going to
ignore the last twenty-five years of US political history? Clinton's
record couldn't be clearer: she and Bill were founding members
of the Democratic Leadership Council. Anti-welfare, anti-single
payer healthcare, pro-banking quote unquote "reform." What's she
progressing to? The whole idea of the neoliberal DLC was to progress
the party *away* from progressive anything.

ELIZABETH

The point is, she'll get things done. There's no point being progressive
if you can't get anything done. She knows how to handle the other
side, to work across the aisle.

LAURA

Handle them? You just heard her. She's touting her record of finding
common ground with them. Have we learnt nothing from the long
wasted years of the Obama administration? I like the aisle. What if
I don't want my president hopping over it to find common ground
with madmen and misanthropes?

Besides, that whole *progressive who likes to get things done* line is a classic centrist put-down of Bernie Sanders and anyone who fancies a bit more serious change than the speaker feels like fighting for. Living wages? Rule of law? Free college? It's a quick and nasty way of dismissing very reasonable things that Americans generally favor by branding them naïve and unrealistic. Peace instead of war? "*You must not like to get things done.*"

Liking to get things done is what killed off single payer health care in the 1990s, before most Americans ever got a chance to vote on it. Bill Clinton got welfare reform done, leaving millions of poor moms in poverty, and criminal justice reform done, sending tens of thousands more to prison. He got NAFTA done over the dead body of the US labor movement. I have no doubt Hillary Clinton will "*get things done.*" The question is, what things?

ELIZABETH

Well, maybe gun control. She's coming on very strong compared to Sanders.

LAURA

Yes, well, now that the candidates have dispensed quickly and breezily with Cooper's cute little question about capitalism vs. socialism— what did Clinton just call inequality, a function of capitalism's excesses? It's not the superfluous sauce; it's the meat and potatoes of the very system. Sanders let the socialist side down on that one.

As for "having to save capitalism from itself," what Clinton just said we "have to do," if I'm not mistaken that's precisely what the bank bailout was supposed to accomplish. A whole lot of Americans didn't think we had to do that. A bipartisan House voted heartily against the idea the first chance they got.[1] Now we have fewer, bigger, richer banks and more poorer people and communities. How's that for combating inequality? At least we saved Goldman to keep paying out those hefty speaking fees to, among others, the Clintons.

ELIZABETH

I'm trying to listen.

(On TV: COOPER: Secretary Clinton, is Bernie Sanders tough enough on guns?
CLINTON: No, not at all. I think we have to look at the fact that we lose ninety people a day from gun violence. This has gone on too long and it's time the entire country stood up against the National Rifle Association …)

ELIZABETH

There you go! You can't complain about that.

LAURA

I'm not complaining, I agree that killing is wrong. I'd just like someone to convey that same message to the Pentagon.

It really is pretty rich for Clinton to pose as the great crusader against violence. I read both of her books, and I don't think she's ever seen a bombing mission she didn't approve of. Hell, Gail Sheehy reports that Hillary broke eighteen months of not speaking to Bill over the Lewinsky affair just to tell him he had to bomb Kosovo. He did. And that's where the whole insidious "humanitarian" war idea got started.

ELIZABETH

Even Bernie Sanders says he approved of those.

LAURA

That doesn't make it right. Killing people to save people? Bombing for democracy? It's been almost unending war since we let that genie out of the interventionists' bottle.

ELIZABETH

She's talking about gun violence. Saying we have to draw a line.

LAURA

Great. I'm just saying that in Newtown, Adam Lanza killed twenty kids, six teachers and his mom and shocked the nation. While Hillary was secretary of state, US weapons killed hundreds, probably thousands of kids in Afghanistan. A single army sergeant methodically slaughtered sixteen civilians, including at least nine kids in their homes one morning. And then there are those drones. Clinton may not personally be there pulling the trigger, but according to the Intercept, she's in the chain of command approving the targets.[2]

A Stanford-NYU study released soon after she left office concluded that from June 2004 through mid-September 2012, drone strikes killed thousands of people, including anything from 474 to 881 civilians and 176 children in Pakistan alone, and we're not even at war with Pakistan! For all the droning on about gun violence, it would be good to hear someone drone on just a bit about drones.[3]

ELIZABETH

Well, at least she's taking on the gun lobby. Calling out the NRA. Holding the gun manufacturers accountable. That takes guts.

LAURA

People are always calling out the NRA. NRA president Wayne
LaPierre came in for no end of grief when he suggested stationing
more shooters in more schools after Newtown. Arm schools to protect
schools? Ridiculous, said all good liberal Dems.

Except that's exactly US foreign policy. When it comes to lobbying for
gun manufacturers, the NRA's only doing what the State Department
does bigger and better. US government-brokered arms sales rose to
a record high while Clinton was secretary of state, to $66.3 billion
dollars, in 2011, more than three-quarters of the global arms market,
driven by major arms deals with Persian Gulf states.[4]

For all the talk of background checks here, when the US approved
a $30 billion deal with Saudi Arabia, it wasn't the background, only
the size of the check that got much attention. In *Hard Choices* she
calls it our "most delicate balancing act" but the fact is, Clinton
knew who she was dealing with. Thanks to WikiLeaks we have the
cable from 2009 where she's writing that Saudi Arabia was—in her
words—"the most significant source of funding to Sunni terrorist
groups worldwide." That's al-Qaeda, the Taliban, you name it.[5] Still,
President Obama said the sale would be good for jobs and the State
Department said that in such an insecure region, the arms deal would
be good for security. How's that different from Wayne LaPierre and
arming schools to make them safer?

ELIZABETH

There aren't a lot of good options.

LAURA

That's exactly what Clinton says! Well here's an easy one: in 2006,
then senator Clinton voted against a bill to ban cluster bombs. Under

Secretary Clinton the US refused to sign an international landmine ban.[6] A problem of bad options? Let me see: join the sane world or back the top brass at the Pentagon who are apparently concerned that if we ban cluster bombs today, tomorrow it could be drones.

Come on! Bernie should offer Clinton to get Vermonters to drop their hunting rifles if whoever is the next president pledges to ban cluster bombs.

ELIZABETH

You're impossible. You think it's easy to be secretary of state? She doesn't have carte blanche to do anything she wants, you know. She has to be tough. At least world leaders respect her. And she makes her points. Incremental change is better than no change. Weren't you in Beijing when she gave that historic speech on women's rights?

LAURA

Yes, she said, "It is a violation of human rights when babies are denied food, or drowned, or suffocated, or their spines broken, simply because they are girls," and not quite a year later her "good friend" and predecessor Madeleine Albright was telling Leslie Stahl that half a million children dying as a result of U.S. sanctions on Iraq was worth the price. "It's worth it!" she said on *60 Minutes*.

So what: it's a violation if you're starved simply because you're a girl, but A-OK if it's simply because you're Iraqi?

ELIZABETH

That's a stretch.

LAURA

No, it's not.

(On TV: SANDERS: I think the secretary is right ... the American people are sick and tired of hearing about your damn emails. CLINTON: Thank you. Me too. Me too. CLINTON, smiling broadly, extends her hand to the senator. They shake and smile.)

ELIZABETH

There, look! She's warm. It doesn't get warmer than that! All that focus on her warmth, her style, her smile. It's just sexism. Those tons of newsprint spent on how warm she is, or not. Why do women always have to be warm anyway? Was Lincoln warm? Was Eisenhower? It's just another double standard. Take that, macho creeps.

LAURA

I entirely agree. When it comes to Clinton, it's not the warmth— it's the wars I have an issue with.

ELIZABETH

Argh!

LAURA

I'm serious. Take everything she just said about what happened in Libya. "Smart power" she calls it. What's so smart about acting without Congress, arming rebels we don't know anything about, and throwing another sovereign state into utter chaos? Even if we did do it from the air *with Arabs.*

The Twittersphere is savaging O'Malley and Webb, but they're
making excellent points here. Webb's totally right. We had no treaties
at stake, no American lives. If it had been Bush and Cheney leading
another NATO assault on another Muslim state, people would be
screaming bloody murder.

ELIZABETH

Republicans *are* screaming bloody murder. What do you think all
those days and days and billions of dollars of partisan committee
hearings on Benghazi are about?

LAURA

Just as Clinton says, they're all about presidential politics. And that's
just as well for her. What we need to be talking about is war and
peace. What Clinton did or didn't say in response to the attack on the
embassy isn't half as important as the unprovoked attack that set the
scene for it. In her book, Clinton calls it "exceptionally complicated,"
but at the very same time that she was pushing for military action
against Libya because that government was using violence to suppress
its opponents, Saudi Arabia was sending thousands of troops into
Bahrain *to support a monarchy doing exactly the same thing.* "Violence
is not and cannot be the answer. A political process is," she told the
crown prince of Bahrain. But apparently violence was and could be a
great answer to the problem of Muammar Gaddafi.[7]

ELIZABETH

I suppose you're going to say "oil interests?"

LAURA

As Sarah Palin would say, *you betcha.* Read the *Washington Post.* Read
Chris Stevens's cables. If the media paid half as much attention to

what Ambassador Stevens said in life as they have paid to his untimely death, oil would at least come in for a mention. He said Gaddafi was getting tougher with US oil companies because the Colonel fancied using more of Libya's wealth for his own purposes—among other things, to fund regional development in order to head off extremist terrorism, and to establish an independent African alternative to the United States' African Command. Cables from the US embassy in Tripoli complain Libya viewed AFRICOM as a "vehicle for latter day colonialism."[8] Imagine!

ELIZABETH

You're not going to argue Muammar Gaddafi was a good guy.

LAURA

The cables show plenty of arms sales going from US manufacturers to Libya *before* 2012. Libyan troops had killed about 400 civilians by the time NATO attacked. The death toll from the bombing will never be known, but it's well over a thousand. NATO missiles managed to kill Gaddafi's son, a twenty-nine-year-old student, and three of his baby grandchildren. If the GOP's going to spend weeks grilling Clinton over Benghazi, it'd be nice if they spent a minute or two asking her about those babies.

(On TV: DON LEMON, with a question from Facebook: Do Black lives matter?)

LAURA

Not if they're Libyan.

ELIZABETH

And the women?

LAURA

War to liberate women. Wasn't that the Bushwoman's line? Look around: The Taliban controls more of Afghanistan than they did in 2001; Iraqi women have been thrown back into the Middle Ages. Clinton went to Tripoli after the Gaddafi regime fell and gave a good lecture on women's rights, but last summer ISIS was busily beheading people on Libya's beaches.[9]

What happened to "you break it, you pay for it?" NATO broke it. Women are paying for it. I just don't get how Hillary Clinton gets to be the beleaguered one in this story.

ELIZABETH

OK, well, I don't know about all that. What I see is that two hours in, Hillary's still the only person up there with a single word to say about women's anything: from early childhood education to women retiring in poverty; paid family leave, equal pay. If she wasn't there, they'd never get mentioned at all.

LAURA

Sure. Fair enough. The guys are so dim about gender, Clinton gets to shine extra bright. That's all well and good. But really. I just wonder, looking to the twenty-first century, if we couldn't find a woman leader who could hold questions of race and gender in her head at the same time. Do we really need another feminist for whom, as Barbara Smith et al. said, *All the women are white and all the Blacks are men*?

Clinton just doesn't seem able to get past that. Take this debate: no mention of women when the subject's police violence and Black lives; no mention of race when the topic switches to gender stuff. How hard would it be, as they say, to connect to #SayHerName?

Clinton just doesn't do it. At least not in public. No standing up for women of color when the sisters were left out of the president's My Brother's Keeper initiative. When she went to Silicon Valley to bemoan sexism in that industry she didn't have a word to say about the racism that's just as rampant. Would a more gender-equal whiteness be ok? She needs to be explicit. She's just lucky none of the radical queer women of Black Lives Matter are asking the questions— *or running for president.* Roll on, twenty-first century!

ELIZABETH

You know she'll get the Black women's vote. And no wonder. Any one of those mad Republicans would be worse than Clinton. Abortion, judges, the Supreme Court. You want Donald Trump in the White House?

LAURA

Here we are again. Abortion. The one woman's issue that's served up to suffice for our vote—as if all the others, from war and wages to the rule of Wall Street, weren't also women's issues. I wonder, what would Democrats have to run on if *Roe* was ever really settled?

(On TV: CLINTON: I can't think of anything more of an outsider than electing the first woman president, but I'm not running because I would be the first woman president. I'm running because I have a lifetime of experience in getting results and fighting for people, fighting for kids, for women, for families, fighting to even the odds. And I know what it takes to get things done.)

ELIZABETH

There she goes! She'll get things done. And she'll be the first woman president. Did you hear that?

LAURA

I did. Twice.

Introduction

Liza Featherstone and Amber A'Lee Frost

Hillary Clinton would be America's first woman president. And for many, that is all she needs to be.

Feminist writer Jessica Valenti declared her fealty as early as 2013, in a *Nation* op-ed titled "Why I'm Voting for Her," illustrated by a silhouette of then secretary of state Hillary Clinton. In a moment of 2008 youthful indiscretion, Valenti admitted, she had voted for Obama, but, she wrote, "this time around I'm voting for a woman ... because I'm fed up." Once Hillary finally announced her candidacy in the spring of 2015, Valenti continued to editorialize in her favor, sticking to the same point: Hillary Clinton is a woman. Valenti was not alone in making this argument, if it could even be called that. Gloria Steinem, icon of second wave feminism, takes every opportunity to proclaim that "it's time!" and that the country is ready. Feminist writer and co-author of *The Book of Jezebel* Kate Harding went with the subtly titled *Dame* magazine think piece, "I Am Voting with My Vagina: Hillary Clinton for President."

Clinton's elevation to feminist-in-chief has been enthusiastic. The level of support from celebrities such as Jennifer Lopez and Beyoncé, endorsements from national feminist organizations, and cheering from the ranks of the Internet make this conclusion seem obvious. A viral phenomenon from Clinton's secretary of state days in 2012 called "Texts from Hillary," using a photo of Clinton looking badass in sunglasses, Blackberry in hand, seated aboard a military plane, is now again revived daily online. Feminist writer Sady Doyle—who describes her politics as well to the left of Clinton but has never wavered in her support—posted one of these memes on her own tumblr in October 2015. Reflecting on the possibility of a Clinton vs. Trump race, she exulted, "Ohhhhhhh, I have so rarely, in my little lifetime, ever, ever, ever been so excited." Lena Dunham, director and creator of the TV series *Girls* and media-anointed voice of millennial women, interviewed Clinton, asking the candidate if she would call herself a feminist. When Clinton answered in the affirmative, Dunham squirmed with irrepressible childlike delight. Given the ecstasy of feminist opinion makers over the low bar of Clinton's gender as sole criteria, we should perhaps not be surprised by their excitement when she began to invoke the f-word. At *The Nation* Katha Pollitt declared herself "excited for Hillary" in June 2015, saying, "Clinton is running as a feminist—and that matters for all women."[1]

But what of those feminists who do not agree? Some mainstream feminists argued away sincere political differences, instead patholo-gizing women who disagreed as neurotic and sad. Gloria Steinem was confident that women who hated Clinton were jealous that her marriage was more egalitarian than theirs—a strange claim given the many public compromises Clinton has made in her relationship with her husband. In her book *My Life on the Road*, Steinem wrote:

> Haters condemn her for staying with her husband despite his well-publicized affairs. It turned out that many of them had suffered

a faithless husband, too, but lacked the ability or the will to leave. They wanted Hillary to punish a powerful man in public on their behalf. I reminded them that presidents from Roosevelt to Kennedy had had affairs, but the haters identified with those first ladies and assumed they couldn't leave. It was Hillary's very strength and independence that made them blame her.

Finally, I resorted to explaining my own reasons for thinking the Clintons just might be, in Shakespeare's phrase, "the marriage of true minds." Yet when I brought this up, some Hillary Haters became even angrier. The fact that Bill valued Hillary as an equal partner—and vice versa—seemed to make them more aware that their own marriages were different ... I began to understand that Hillary represented the very public, in-your-face opposite of the precarious and unequal lives that some women were living. In a classic sense, they were trying to kill the messenger.[2]

Then again, in early February 2016, Gloria Steinem explained the Hillary campaign's lower poll numbers among young women than those of her socialist opponent, Senator Bernie Sanders, via the bizarrely sexist suggestion that they were flocking to be "where the boys are"—discrediting their political agency, painting them instead as under informed and merely infatuated. She later apologized, calling it a moment of "talk show interruptus" and bad editing, but it is apparent that critical feminist analysis comes secondary to a certain class of feminist groupthink.

This has long been true: over the course of Clinton's political career, commentators have suggested that women voters felt intimidated by her and everything she had accomplished. Still other so-called feminists have been willing to throw even more basic principles under the bus to back their girl. Back when then intern Monica Lewinsky famously gave Bill Clinton a blow job in the Oval Office, a roundtable of prominent feminists in the *New York Observer* made fun of her looks, implied that she was stupid and slut-shamed her. Nancy Friday even suggested that Lewinsky "rent out her mouth."[3] None of this was Hillary Clinton's fault—she did call Lewinsky a "narcissistic loony tune," but it was a private conversation and one can understand her annoyance—but the fact that establishment feminists were willing to say such deeply misogynist things about a young woman with no power revealed just the sort of feminism that Hillary represents: one that is for insiders only.

Many more feminists claimed that liberal and left men who criticized Clinton just didn't like women. Joan Walsh complained that Clinton-haters sound like "they're talking about Glenn Close in *Fatal Attraction*."[4] After the first Democratic debate, such Hillary stalwarts were outraged by the sexism of anyone who was impressed by the performance of Senator Bernie Sanders. A blogger at the Daily Kos saw a vast somewhere-out-there conspiracy: "Hillary can't even win a debate without being told she sucks by the Internet."[5] Amanda Marcotte wrote a column for Salon equating the "silly sexism" of the "lefty smartypants crowd" with that of Fox News.[6]

Such a way of thinking could only be accepted in a public discourse that has a limited understanding of feminism and its function, blithely deploying gender politics to boost the status quo. But capital-F Feminism is not an anatomical Super Bowl in which all adherents root for Team Vagina.

Instead, feminism is a set of political ideas, or several sets of political ideas that are often wildly at odds. This book itself advances a vociferous disagreement with the type of feminism that has produced and sustained Hillary Rodham Clinton. While she is indeed a woman, she also, as Kathleen Geier observes in this book, served as the first (and at the time, only) woman on the board of Walmart, a company that has systematically discriminated against its low-wage female employees for decades. As the largest private employer in the nation, Walmart employs 1.4 million people in the US and 2.2 million worldwide. Although the company boasts a majority female workforce of "associates" (making it the largest employer of women in the country), it's a notoriously wretched company for women, built on horrifying labor practices worldwide, including sweatshops overseas, wage and promotion discrimination, wage theft, sexual harassment, cuts to hours, wrongful termination, and abysmal benefits and pay. There is no evidence that Clinton ever attempted to seriously address the problems faced by low-wage female workers during her time with the company, and she has always declined to give interviews on this subject.[7]

Clinton once said: "As a shareholder and director of our company, I'm always proud of Wal-Mart and what we do and the way we do it better than anybody else."[8] Meanwhile interviewers like Lena Dunham never ask her about such relationships, which might disrupt the lovefest of giggles and retweets that serve to make us all feel good about electing a woman president.

Sure, as Amanda Marcotte and others have been quick to point out, Clinton is talking about feminist issues like family leave on the campaign trail. She has "introduced herself" to the American people many times over—reminiscent of that important person at the cocktail party who never seems to remember you've, in fact, met before—but this time around, she is doing so more explicitly as a feminist. But her entire record suggests that she is bad news for women—and for that matter, most of us who are not part of the Hollywood, Washington, or global financial elite.

The writers in this collection know that record very well.

Clinton was instrumental in her husband's decision to deprive poor women and children of the basic social safety net that welfare once provided, as Frances Fox Piven and Fred Block note in their essay for this collection. In interviews, Clinton has described women struggling to raise their children on welfare as unproductive "deadbeats,"[9] as contributor Amber A'Lee Frost observes in these pages. In Arkansas while Bill was governor, Hillary played a crucial role, as Megan Erickson shows, in demonizing public school teachers—many of them African American women—and dismantling their unions, a sexist and racist tactic that succeeded then and has set the tone in the continuing American political debates over education.

But Hillary Clinton hasn't just been bad for American women. As secretary of state, she lobbied to ensure that Haitian women toiling in garment factories would not receive an increase in the minimum wage, because American corporate interests objected. As Belén Fernández argues in this collection, Secretary Clinton's indulgence of and behind-the-scenes assistance to an undemocratic coup in Honduras is responsible for a dramatic increase in murder—and yes, femicide—in that country and the profound social destabilization that inevitably follows each incident of American imperialism. At a time when younger feminists, and even mainstream human rights groups like Amnesty International, were questioning the logic of punitive approaches to sex work that only endanger those who work in the sex trade, Hillary Rodham Clinton's State Department was actively rewarding such policies, even punishing those groups who wouldn't go along, as Margaret Corvid argues.

Medea Benjamin, founder of the direct action group CODEPINK, describes in her chapter a warmongering secretary of state, whose policies perpetuated violence—including rape and femicide—in the Middle East. While many have resisted, on both feminist and plain empirical grounds, any suggestion that women are inherently peaceful, there has long been a robust feminist anti-war tradition, from Virginia Woolf's book *Three Guineas* to Women Strike for Peace in the 1950s to, more recently, CODEPINK itself. This tradition emerges from a principled opposition to state violence but also from a critique of the kind of masculinity that rewards war and imperialism. Feminists supporting Hillary Clinton are willfully overlooking her war record and choosing to reject that deeply humane tradition.

Clinton has advanced feminism, yes. Just by standing up and insisting on staying in public life, despite all the right-wing misogynist attacks, she has been an important icon to many women, a symbol of decades of changing gender norms. And in 1995, as first lady, she made history by declaring at the United Nations Fourth World Congress on Women in Beijing, "women's rights are human rights." But hers is the kind of feminism that, as Yasmin Nair and Donna Murch point out in their essays for this collection, has also advanced the punitive policies that have led to our current mass incarceration crisis, often in the name of protecting women and children. As this book went to press, Black Lives Matters protesters had just interrupted a Clinton speech in Atlanta and been escorted out of the room. Clinton's feminism is the sort that only benefits a handful of wealthy, white Americans—most saliently Hillary Clinton herself.

Senator Bernie Sanders, the only American politician of national stature who calls himself a socialist, is at the time of this writing still running a visible and popular primary challenge to Clinton. He is better than Clinton not only on economic issues, but also on reproductive choice and gay rights. Yet our liberal chattering classes frame the choice between Sanders and Clinton as a choice between democratic socialism and feminism—and the two are assumed to be incompatible. At a feminist bookstore event in late October 2015, Gloria Steinem repeated her enthusiasm for Clinton and noted pityingly that Sanders was an "old-fashioned socialist." She liked him for it but added, "He's not my candidate."[10] Salon's Amanda Marcotte did her best to portray Bernie Sanders as the favored candidate of creepy misogynists on Reddit, and dubbed his supporters a "he-man woman haters club," ignoring the thousands of women showing up at his events around the country and the 44 percent of female New Hampshire Democratic primary voters who intended to vote for him, according to a December 2015 poll (just one percentage point behind his far more famous rival).[11]

We thus see in Clinton's campaign a new, troubling era in which feminism, now a proper media subject, is used rhetorically as a cudgel against any sort of left politics which might actually help the vast majority of women. We saw this recently in the UK as well, with the liberal campaign against democratic socialist Jeremy Corbyn in 2015 denouncing him for being little more than an old white man, even though his female challengers were politically far to his right.

Why should socialism and feminism be incompatible? This persistent framing shows how horribly both feminism and the left have failed to make the case that for the vast majority of the world's women, liberation *requires* socialism, or something much like it.

Not all the contributors to this volume support Bernie Sanders in his campaign, and almost surely, each of them would find fault with him, especially on foreign policy. But there is no doubt that most women have more to gain even from Sanders's watered-down social democracy than from the ruthless neoliberalism that Clinton represents. As they compose the majority of college students, women stand to gain immeasurably from making college tuition debt-free, as Sanders advocates, far more than from the tepid tinkering on the issue in Clinton's platform. Sanders's attention to living wages and the creation of decently paying jobs and single payer health care, as well as his focus on economic inequality, has the potential to speak to almost everyone, but women especially, since women make up the majority of low-wage workers and head the majority of households below the poverty line. Gender and economic justice are deeply intertwined, and it is embarrassing how easily Americans get distracted from this fact. Sanders' platform also has plenty to say on gendered matters like abortion rights and equal pay—he even mentions the storied Equal Rights Amendment, subject of a decades-long feminist battle for ratification.

To her credit, unlike so many of her supporters, Hillary Clinton has not argued that she deserves to be president more than Sanders *solely* because she would be the first woman. She has played that card, but who wouldn't? The first woman president would indeed be historically significant. But Clinton has not reduced the race to one of anatomy; instead, she has argued in vigorous defense of the destructive politics she represents. She claimed in the first Democratic primary debate of the 2016 election cycle, held in October 2015, that capitalism was better than socialism, and memorably pointed out that the United States is "not Denmark." Indeed, it is not: almost all Denmark's social indicators—poverty, food security, happiness—are better than ours. With this dramatic remark, Clinton made clear that Americans should vote for her if they prefer a child poverty rate higher than that of any wealthy country besides Romania.

The writers and thinkers in this book will probably persuade you—if you're not already convinced—that Hillary Clinton doesn't represent a promising sort of feminism. But perhaps more importantly, these writers offer a glimpse of a feminism beyond Hillary, a set of politics critical of the harsh, capitalist, warmongering, punitive, and compassion-free policies to which she has devoted her career.

Let the rest of the punditocracy, ordained feminists among them, yawn and dismiss left ideas as "old" or "unrealistic." Meanwhile, people around the world remain outraged at and suffering under the deprivation created by the extractive, neoliberal style of government that benefits only millionaires like Hillary Clinton. In recent years, long after Clinton's stint at Walmart, workers there have slowly been improving their conditions by organizing. That's the kind of feminism represented in this book—a left feminism rooted in an understanding of women's material conditions. Our kind of feminism will outlive Hillary Clinton. But we must work hard to make sure it triumphs over the ruling class feminism that she represents.

PART I: HILLARY AT HOME

ONE

Hillary Clinton, Economic Populist:
Are You Fucking Kidding Me?

Kathleen Geier

I n 1998, then first lady Hillary Clinton requested a meeting with
Elizabeth Warren. At the time a Harvard law professor, Warren
had written a *New York Times* op-ed denouncing a bankruptcy
"reform" bill that would have forced debtors to prioritize credit
card payments over child support. In their meeting, Warren proved
extremely persuasive, so much so that at its conclusion Clinton
announced, "Professor Warren, we've got to stop that awful bill."[1]
Warren was elated, certain she'd made a convert. And President Bill
Clinton did indeed end up vetoing the bill.

But this repulsive piece of legislation wasn't dead yet. In 2001,
the same "awful bill" was re-introduced in Congress. And this time,
Hillary Clinton, now the newly elected senator from New York,
voted in its favor.

It was a betrayal that Elizabeth Warren never forgot; she mentioned
it as recently as her 2012 Senate campaign. In her 2003 book, *The
Two-Income Trap*, Warren acidly noted that Bill Clinton "was a lame

duck at the time he vetoed the bill; he could afford to forgo future campaign contributions. As New York's newest senator, however, it seems that Hillary Clinton could not afford such a principled position."[2]

As Hillary Clinton campaigns for president, the media is talking up her so-called "populism." But as this story so aptly illustrates, Clinton has never been a reliable champion of the economic interests of working people. On the contrary, from Arkansas and the White House through the US Senate and the State Department, one thing has been crushingly obvious: catering to the demands of Wall Street and other economic elites has always been her prime objective.

> *"For goodness' sake, you can't be a lawyer if you don't represent banks."*
>
> —Hillary Clinton, on the campaign trail in 1992[3]

Ideologically, Hillary Clinton has always been a chameleon. In 1964, the teenaged Hillary was much taken with Barry Goldwater, the right-wing extremist presidential candidate, but by 1969, she had gone full hippie. In a graduation speech she delivered at Wellesley that year, she gushed: "There are some things we feel, feelings that our prevailing, acquisitive, and competitive corporate life, including tragically the universities, is not the way of life for us. We're searching for more immediate, ecstatic, and penetrating modes of living."[4] Groovy! For a short period after, her inchoate critiques of capitalism continued. In a 1970 talk before the League of Women Voters, she railed, "How much longer can we let corporations run us?"[5]

But Hillary was young, and it was the '60s. As soon as the political winds shifted, Hillary was quick to trim her sails. After brief stints working in government (nine months on the Watergate-era House Judiciary Committee), academia (a few semesters teaching at the School of Law at the University of Arkansas, Fayetteville), and the nonprofit sector (less than a year at the Children's Defense Fund), she set her sights elsewhere. The pivotal moment came in 1977, when she joined the Rose Law Firm of Little Rock, Arkansas, a politically powerful corporate practice whose clients included such unsavory economic players as Walmart, Tyson Foods, and Monsanto. Her biographers record no evidence that Hillary's abrupt transition from civic-minded do-goodism to corporate hackwork occasioned her a single dark night of the soul—or even much cognitive dissonance. Biographer Carl Bernstein even suggests that Hillary had the opportunity to join the state's largest public interest law firm but chose Rose instead.

Though her campaign biography plays up the pro bono work she performed at Rose, the vast majority of her working hours were dedicated to her corporate clients. In one early case, Clinton, representing local businesses, filed suit against the community-organizing group, ACORN, which had helped pass a ballot measure that lowered electricity costs for residential users but raised commercial rates. That particular legal dispute goes unmentioned in Clinton's memoir, *Living History*, but she does touch on some of her smaller corporate cases. She describes her defense of a canning company against a plaintiff who found a rat's ass in his pork and beans and her representation of a logging company accused of negligence in an accident that maimed several workers. She frames these cases as lighthearted anecdotes, highlighting their comic grotesqueries rather than the sleazy actions of her corporate clients. This was the kind of legal work she performed dutifully for fifteen years, which would turn out to be the longest she'd work for any single employer.

During her years at the Rose Law Firm, Clinton also took home a tidy sum—over a third of her income[6]—sitting on the boards of corporations including TCBY (the frozen yogurt company), LaFarge (a cement manufacturer), and, most famously, Walmart. In the six years she served on the Walmart board, she never once spoke up in defense of labor unions for the company's majority-female workforce. Yet during that period (1986–1992), Walmart was ruthlessly suppressing workers' organizing efforts, and at board meetings, one of Walmart's honchos was fond of saying charming things like "Labor unions are nothing but blood-sucking parasites living off the productive labor of people who work for a living."[7] Walmart's war on unions, like its discrimination against women, goes unmentioned in her memoir. But she does manage to coo about how Sam Walton taught her "a great deal about business integrity and success."[8]

At the Clinton White House, Hillary was not exactly known as a tribune of the working class. She helped craft her husband's "triangulation" strategy and supported his least populist economic policies, including the North American Free Trade Agreement (NAFTA), which resulted in plummeting working class wages and the loss of more than 682,000 American jobs,[9] as well the Commodity Futures Modernization Act, which exempted credit default swaps from regulation and helped unleash the Great Recession of 2007–2009. In 2000, when she won a US Senate seat, her liberal supporters breathed a sigh of relief. At long last, they imagined, an independent Hillary would be "liberated" to be her true, supposedly lefty self.

But that, of course, was a fantasy. Even though she was representing a relatively liberal state, her centrist orientation remained. While Hillary voted with the Democrats on most economic issues, there were notable occasions when she veered sharply to the right of party consensus.[10] In addition to the bankruptcy vote that so deeply disappointed Elizabeth Warren, Clinton supported several measures that favored agribusiness and big oil, backed a law that would have slashed estate taxes, and voted for the massive 2008 bailout bill that rescued the banks but failed to hold them accountable.

At the next stop in her political career, the State Department, Clinton continued to shill tirelessly on behalf of American corporations. As the *Wall Street Journal* put it, Hillary "redefined the [Secretary of State] job in ways that promoted the interests of U.S. business." Among recent secretaries of state, said the *Journal*, Hillary was "one of the most aggressive global cheerleaders for American companies," lobbying foreign governments to "sign deals and change policies to the advantage of corporate giants" such as General Electric, Exxon Mobil, Boeing, and Microsoft.[11]

Clinton's rationale for her business-oriented diplomacy was that it was good for the American economy. Though that's highly debatable, one thing is certain: these deals were very good indeed for Hillary Clinton. According to a *Wall Street Journal* analysis, at least sixty companies that lobbied the State Department during her tenure as secretary donated over $26 million to the nonprofit Clinton Foundation. In addition, forty-four of those firms made additional donations totaling a cool $3.2 billion to the Clinton Global Initiative, one of the foundation's offshoots. In several instances—as when she advocated for Walmart in India, and General Electric in Algeria—the timing between Hillary's lobbying for a particular firm and that same firm's foundation contributions is suspiciously close.[12]

While Clinton's tenure at State was a bonanza to many of the world's largest multinational corporations, labor was not so lucky. Take, for example, the free trade pact with Colombia. During her 2008 presidential run, Clinton opposed the proposed agreement, citing concerns about violence against trade union workers. But two years later, after the Canadian petro giant Pacific Rubiales donated millions of dollars to the Clinton Foundation, she reversed herself. Pacific Rubiales has operations in Colombia and was aggressively backing the measure. Human rights and labor groups identified Pacific Rubiales as the chief instigator of anti-labor violence and protested the threats, attacks, and even murders of union members that had continued unabated, in clear violation of the trade pact. (The company has denied these charges.) Even so, Clinton's State

Department repeatedly declared that the country was compliant with human rights standards and never investigated the charges against Pacific Rubiales. In spite of activists' many pleas, Clinton and company took no action to stop the anti-labor persecutions in Colombia.[13]

The Clinton Foundation, which has played a central role in consolidating and extending the Clintons' power and influence, has been controversial for good reasons. The foundation's defenders point to its global work fighting the spread of AIDS. But it has also been charged with providing Haiti with "shoddy and dangerous" emergency shelters.[14]

Notwithstanding its humanitarian projects, the foundation's most important function appears to be as a handy vehicle for influence peddling on a massive scale. Not only does a donation enable rich and powerful firms or individuals to burnish their (often deservedly tarnished) public image, it buys them access to, and influence over, a former secretary of state and potential future president. In turn, the receipt of the donation cements the ties between the Clintons and rich and powerful corporations and individuals—the better for future fundraising efforts, especially campaign donations. Moreover, the foundation provides global political elites and economic elites with unprecedented opportunities to network, bond, and expand the scope of their power and influence. Everybody wins, right?

Everyone, that is, except the 99 percent, who aren't in on the hustle. They might prefer that we solve problems of global poverty and inequality through bottom-up political movements and democratic governance, as opposed to top-down, unaccountable charities that depend on the whims of the rich. And they surely have reason to feel uneasy about Big Philanthropy institutions like the Clinton Foundation, which by their very structure provide endless opportunities for elite muckraking and influence peddling, thus consolidating the global domination of the 1 percent.

"One of my favorite people in the administration, [former Treasury Secretary and Goldman Sachs co-chair] Bob [Rubin] is fabulously smart and successful, yet thoroughly self-effacing."
—Hillary Clinton in her memoir
Living History (2003)

Hillary Clinton has terrible taste in men.

I'm not so much talking about Bill (though there's that), but the men in her professional life. Many of Hillary's closest political aides have been men from the elite strata of finance and the corporate world, who have served neither her nor the country particularly well. At the beginning of the Clinton administration, Bill Clinton tasked his wife with reforming the American health care system; Hillary chose as her chief advisor, not a health policy expert, activist, or experienced political leader, but business consultant Ira Magaziner. Magaziner proved spectacularly ill equipped for his role. As economist Brad DeLong has argued, Magaziner's technocratic approach and penchant for secrecy, which served him well in the corporate consulting world, turned out to be disastrous in a political context, where reaching out and building coalitions are key.[15] The campaign to enact Hillarycare ended in catastrophic defeat, and it would be another two decades before anyone took a crack at seriously reforming the American health care system. In the interim, countless uninsured Americans needlessly lost their health, their savings, and their lives.

By far the most troubling of Hillary's associations are her close, cozy, and long-standing ties to Wall Street and the banks. That's because our bloated financial sector is at the heart of so much of the economic dysfunction and injustice in our society. Because Wall Street habitually encourages the misallocation of capital into speculative rather than productive investments, our economy has suffered from sluggish growth. Financialization has also been a major driver of inequality, as deregulation has shifted rents to financial elites, bringing on soaring executive compensation on Wall Street and elsewhere.[16] Finally, financialization has spurred asset bubbles, which have in turn led to severe financial crises, such as the housing bubble that precipitated the Great Recession.

If you wanted to identify the single individual most responsible for the financialization of the American economy, you might pick Robert Rubin. As Clinton's treasury secretary, he adamantly opposed the regulation of derivatives and aggressively advocated for the repeal of laws such as the Gramm-Leach-Bliley Act that had long separated investment banks from their commercial counterparts. These policy changes were among the chief causes of the worldwide financial meltdown and recession of 2007–2009. In the private sector, Rubin's actions were equally catastrophic. At Citi, he aggressively urged the bank to take on more risk.[17] That approach drove Citi into insolvency, contributed to millions of Americans losing their jobs and homes, and led to years of economic misery on a global scale. But it didn't stop Rubin from hoovering up a cool $126 million during his decade-long tenure at Citi.[18]

Carl Bernstein reports that at the outset of the Clinton administration, Rubin took it upon himself to "tutor" Hillary in economic policy. Hillary's memoir confirms that the two developed a warm relationship and were generally in ideological sympathy. As Rubin recounted in his memoir *In an Uncertain World*, early in Clinton's presidency he argued that it was "inadvisable" for the administration to use "class-laden language" to sell its economic plan. He wrote, "Even talking about 'the rich,' it seemed to me, had an unnecessary normative connotation, suggesting that there was something wrong with having been successful financially." Alarmed, he notified Hillary:

Hillary not only agreed, she marched me down to the Roosevelt Room, where Paul Begala was working on the speech. She stood over Paul's shoulder as he rephrased the problematic passages.[19]

Another key economic debate took place right after the 1994 midterms, when, as Rubin relates, the administration argued over "whether to take a more populist or a more centrist tack." Secretary of Labor Robert Reich championed a populist approach. Rubin fiercely opposed him, arguing that if the administration used words like "corporate welfare," it "could adversely affect the business confidence requisite for economic growth." Hillary took Rubin's side in the debate. According to Rubin, she told Reich, "Bob, the polls and political intelligence we have say that the people we need to reach don't respond well to that kind of approach."[20] Rubin's pupil had learned her lessons well.

And so have most other powerful Democrats. The outsized influence of the financial sector is not merely a personal issue, unique to Hillary Clinton, but a structural problem affecting the entire Democratic Party. So-called Rubinomics—which, in a nutshell, consists of bailouts and upward redistribution for the rich, a few crumbs for the poor (remember Clinton-era "micro-initiatives" like midnight basketball?), and practically nothing to strengthen labor or rein in capital—has been the dominant Democratic doctrine for decades now. Rubin has a reputation as a Democratic kingmaker and éminence grise. The tentacles of his power extend throughout the party, via the many (white) (men) whom he's mentored and who hold similar neoliberal views. His fingerprints are all over the past two Democratic administrations. The last three Democratic secretaries of the treasury, Larry Summers, Tim Geithner, and Jack Lew, have all been Rubin protégés.

Since the 2007 financial meltdown, neoliberalism in general and Rubin's reputation in particular have lost much of their former luster. Nevertheless, Rubin continues to be a major behind-the-scenes

Democratic power broker. He was an adviser to Hillary during her 2008 campaign, and as the *New York Times* reported in 2014, he "will play an essential role in Hillary Rodham Clinton's campaign for president in 2016."[21]

Although Wall Street caused the most devastating financial crisis since the Great Depression, financial elites maintain a tight grip on the Democrats' economic policy apparatus. And based on her record and political ties, there is little reason to believe that President Hillary Clinton would reverse her party's long, inexorable march rightward on economic issues.

> *"Senator Obama's support among working, hard-working Americans, white Americans, is weakening again, and [...] whites in both states who had not completed college [are] supporting me."*
>
> —Hillary Clinton in an interview with *USA Today*, 2008

In her presidential campaign, Hillary is trying to have it both ways. In private, she has shamelessly courted the financial sector; and certainly, she continues to feel the Wall Street love ("Why Wall Street Loves Hillary" blared a November 2014 Politico headline).

At the same time, however, she is publicly striking a populist pose. Much of the media, including the *Washington Post* ("Clinton Strikes Populist Tone in Long-Awaited Campaign Announcement," April 12, 2015), the *New York Times* ("Hillary Clinton's Vows to 'Fight' Evoke a Populist Appeal," June 15, 2015), CNN ("Clinton Strikes Populist Tone to Make Case for 2016 Campaign," June 13, 2015), and *Time* magazine ("Hillary Clinton Launches Her Campaign as Economic Populist," June 13, 2015), has been happy to go along with the populist charade. But populism, at least as we normally define it—a political doctrine that supports the interests of ordinary people over those of privileged elites—has never been a component of Hillary's political DNA. Her public career, from Arkansas to the White House to the Senate to the State Department, has rarely been characterized by populist policies or even populist rhetoric.

It is no wonder that, according to Politico, "on Wall Street, they don't believe [Hillary's populism] for a minute." One financial insider told Politico that the Street is "very excited about Hillary," because they "have confidence that she understands how things work and that she's not a populist."[22]

Her "populism" is mostly a product of election year expediency. Hillary conveniently discovered populism in the middle of her 2008 primaries, when she realized she was losing the presidential contest to Barack Obama. Early in that campaign, she had unapologetically defended lobbyists, admonishing an audience of liberal bloggers that "lobbyists, whether you like it or not, represent real Americans." But by March the next year, the Ivy-educated ex-corporate lawyer had morphed into (in Gail Sheehy's words) "hardscrabble Hillary," the self-proclaimed granddaughter of a Scranton mill hand who was vowing to "take on" credit card companies, health insurers, the pharmaceutical industry, and even Wall Street—albeit in ways that were left mostly unspecified.[23] There followed a cascade of "woman of the people" photo opportunities: Hillary posing at gas pumps and pickup trucks, or downing a beer and a shot with blue-collar types. In this, she was imitating the kind of class masquerade perfected by rich Republicans from Ronald Reagan to George W. Bush (recall Reagan's ranch, George H. W.'s pork rinds, and other such moments). Her populist play-acting was for the benefit of the white working class, whose votes she craved. As such it had uncomfortable racist undertones, hence her tone-deaf comments about "hardworking Americans, white Americans." For Clinton, populism was an awkward fit at best.

For the 2016 election, with the electorate in a restive mood, Clinton has gone back to the populist well. Her rhetoric is more left wing than last time. She talks about paid family leave and increasing Social Security and the minimum wage, all welcome developments. Yet there is little substance behind the speechifying.

Take, for instance, the much-touted speech on the economy she delivered in July 2015, which turned out to be a big bowl of luke-warm mush.[24] The rhetoric was bland, and the proposals were light on details. She called for an increase in the minimum wage, but didn't say how much; supported paid family leave, but offered no specifics about how it would work.

She did vow to "empower entrepreneurs" through failed poli-cies such as "empowerment zones" (a Reagan-era scam in which inner city businesses were showered with goodies like tax giveaways and exemptions from minimum wage, purportedly to stimulate economic development). In this important campaign speech, she inexplicably wasted verbiage on this bogus policy. Yet on many of the most urgent economic issues of our time, Clinton remained silent.

Clinton didn't call for breaking up the big banks or enacting a financial transactions tax. She said nothing about the Federal Reserve or the vital importance of the frequently ignored component of that organization's "dual mandate": maximum employment. She alluded to a "sharing economy," but there were no proposals about how to regulate it to avoid rampant labor exploitation. She said little about fiscal policy, and nothing about expanding workers' right to organ-ize. Most curiously in a supposedly populist speech, there were no fiery denunciations of the rich and powerful, nor a whisper of criti-cism of Wall Street for vaporizing the global economy.

She did, however, take time to mention how much she enjoys being a grandmother.

Clinton's plan for reforming Wall Street, released some months after that economic speech, was equally underwhelming, more tweaks than overhaul. James Kwak, an academic who specializes in financial markets and regulation, described it as "a laundry list of marginally better-than-nothing reforms that are likely to vanish into an abyss of rule-writing and regulatory dithering."[25]

There was a good reason why Clinton's speech was so thin: Wall Street wanted it that way. Politico reported that Clinton "had been reaching out to [financial sector] executives to preview the message" and that it was carefully crafted to include nothing that "would freak people [on Wall Street] out." What, exactly, would panic them, then? According to Politico's source, such policies would include "a big financial transactions test; bigger capital requirements; breaking up the biggest banks; raising capital gains rates." The source claimed that any rhetoric "[s]hort of these policy proposals ... doesn't really mean anything," adding, "She's going to talk left but so far her policies are mostly just center-left."[26]

That Clinton gives Wall Street the veto power over her economic agenda makes sense if you follow the money. The heads of Goldman Sachs, Morgan Stanley, JPMorgan Chase, and Bank of America all support her candidacy, and five of her top ten donors for 2016 are financial services firms.[27] Over the past two decades, Bill and Hillary Clinton have raised over $1 billion in campaign donations from US companies and corporate executives, and among these, the sector that was the single biggest source of funds was financial services.[28] By contrast, donations from labor unions during this period came to $40 million—about 0.04 percent of the contributions of business interests. Those numbers tell us everything we need to know about the Clintons' priorities.

> *"We came out of the White House not only dead broke, but in debt."*
> —Hillary Clinton in an interview with Diane Sawyer, 2014

In addition to her associations, public record, and positions on the issues, Hillary's attempt to reinvent herself as an economic populist

faces yet another stumbling block: the Clintons' extraordinary
wealth. If nominated, Hillary will become one of the wealthiest
Democratic standard-bearers in history; if elected, she will become
one of the richest presidents of all time. According to a 2014
analysis, Bill Clinton is the ninth richest president in American
history, as measured by peak net worth, making him substantially
more affluent than Reagan or either of the Bushes (not to mention
Nixon, Ford, and Carter).[29] The Clintons' loot put them not just
in the top 1 percent of the income distribution, but the top 0.01
percent.[30]

The Clintons' thirst for money seems bottomless. Since leaving
office, they have become spectacularly wealthy from their book deals
and speaking fees. Between January 2014 and May 2015 alone, the
Clintons earned over $30 million, including more than $25 million
for 104 speeches, many of them for public universities and other
not-for-profit organizations.[31] The Clintons donated some of their
speaking fees to their favorite charity: the Clinton Foundation, in
case there was any doubt. Even so, Hillary kept approximately $11
million of the money she earned from speechmaking during that
period.[32] According to publicly available financial records, that sum
stayed in her personal account and was not donated.

Hillary's average fee for a single speech is around $225,000, or
more than four times the median household income in the US.[33] In
addition, the terms of Hillary's standard speaking contract demand
nothing less than luxury hotel accommodations for herself and her
entourage, plus travel in a $39 million, 16-passenger Gulfstream
G450 jet.[34] The Clintons aren't royalty, rock stars, or Hollywood
legends. But they certainly live like them, which gives the lie to
Hillary's populist schtick—particularly when she's trying to persuade the American public that she's just like the rest of us. Hillary
told Diane Sawyer that upon leaving the White House, she and Bill
were "dead broke," but in fact, a few weeks before their exit, they
bought themselves a house for a cash down payment of $855,000

plus a $1.995 million mortgage. Clearly, being "dead broke" ain't what it used to be.[35]

As a former president and first lady, the Clintons are supposed to be, first and foremost, public servants. Their power is a public trust, bestowed by the people who democratically elected them, with the understanding that they use it for the common good. Instead, they have pursued personal enrichment to an unparalleled degree—no other ex-president has done anything like this.

But if you consider the Clintons' wealth in the context of the glitzy, jet-setting Davos types that are their peer group, amassing such indecent amounts of it looks like their equivalent of keeping up with the Joneses. To a degree unlike any other presidential candidate that has come before her, Hillary Clinton has spent nearly a quarter of a century at the commanding heights of the global elite, on a nonstop schedule of fundraisers, summits, and other events where she is constantly rubbing shoulders with the world's wealthiest and most powerful people: financiers, CEOs, celebrities, world leaders, heirs to great fortunes. Even Bill and Hillary's own flesh and blood belongs to this economic elite: Chelsea Clinton put in a stint at an investment bank, and her husband, Marc Mezvinsky, manages a $400 million hedge fund.[36] When you have immersed yourself in the waters of extreme affluence so deeply, and for so long, it tends to shape your worldview.

Then there's the impact that such a cavernous economic divide between voters and the elected officials who represent them has had on our democracy. A growing body of research has documented stark class divisions on economics, with the wealthy being notably hostile to the kinds of economic policies—more social spending, guaranteed jobs, an increase in the minimum wage, higher taxes on the rich—that low- and middle-income Americans strongly support.[37] Compounding the problem is that policymakers tend to be fawningly attentive to the preferences of their fellow elites, while ignoring everyone else. In a recently published study, political scientists Martin Gilens and Benjamin Page found that "the preferences of the average American appear to have only a minuscule, near-zero, statistically nonsignificant impact upon public policy."[38] Campaign finance in the post–*Citizens United* climate has only strengthened the hand of the rich. An August 2015 *New York Times* analysis showed that nearly half the money raised for the 2016 presidential election is from fewer than 158 families, a concentration of political donors that it called "unprecedented in the modern era."[39]

But it's not only through lobbying or campaign donations that the wealthy dominate our politics. Something more subtle is going on. The socioeconomic similarities between political elites and economic elites are growing, so much so that the two groups are becoming indistinguishable. Millionaires are only 3 percent of the population, but they constitute strong majorities of the Senate, the House of Representatives, and the Supreme Court (not to mention the men in the White House). No wonder they are so sympathetic to the claims of the upper class—particularly when it comes to the most crucial political decisions, the ones that take place behind closed doors.

The Clintons' many apologists would likely shrug their shoulders at Bill and Hillary's deep ties to the global financial elite. They'd insist there is no alternative to Clinton-style neoliberalism and that resistance is both childish and futile. The only changes we can make, they'd argue, are incremental ones—nudges and tweaks. And even enacting those requires the endless stroking and appeasement of the 1 percent, who after all have the power and the money not only to buy elections, but also to destroy, or at least seriously enfeeble, any proposed reforms (the crippling of the Dodd-Frank financial regulations being a recent case in point). The best hope for human progress, then, lies in sitting back and letting political elites slavishly cultivate moneyed interests, who then might deign to let us enact a few micro-initiatives. Midnight basketball for everyone!

But such pragmatism has shriveled the imagination of the left. It has defanged and demobilized a generation of activists and has ended up entrenching even more deeply the odious system that it purports to reform.

On economics, candidate Hillary is running to the left not only of her own husband, but also Barack Obama. That sounds encouraging, until you consider that Clinton's back is against the wall, as she is under immense political pressure coming from an increasingly left-leaning Democratic base and a surprisingly strong challenge from Bernie Sanders, the only US senator to call himself a socialist. If the left can keep the political heat on, perhaps President Hillary will make good on her election-year promises to enact paid family leave, higher Social Security benefits, and other redistributive policies. But that seems doubtful; to the left, Clinton has been a fair-weather friend at best. When facing political adversity, her deepest instincts are to tack to the right.

Regardless of Hillary Clinton's election-year posturing, she cannot be trusted to follow through. That was a political lesson that Elizabeth Warren learned long ago. It's long past time that the rest of us take it to heart.

TWO

Ending Poverty as We Know It

Frances Fox Piven and Fred Block

In 2014 the US Census reported that 45.3 million people, or 14.5 percent of the population, lived on incomes that made them officially poor. International comparisons suggest an even higher US poverty rate (17.9 percent in 2012) and that makes the US the leader in poverty among the rich countries of the world.[1] Most troubling of all are indications that extreme poverty, defined as the number of households living with incomes less than half of the federal poverty line, has been increasing rapidly over the last fifteen years, and such extreme poverty households include close to 3 million children.[2]

Yet these levels of poverty receive almost no attention in our national political debates. Conservatives continue to insist that programs such as food stamps and unemployment insurance are abused by welfare cheaters. The left defends these programs but timidly, preferring proposals to alleviate poverty by raising the minimum wage and creating more jobs.

But we can use Hillary Clinton's history with the issue of poverty as a cautionary tale about the dangers of trying to address poverty by focusing on labor market reforms. Clinton began her career as a lawyer in the late 1970s working with Marion Wright Edelman's poverty advocacy organization, The Children's Defense Fund.

But by the time she popularized the slogan "It takes a village" to raise a child, in her 1996 book of that title, this sort of liberalism was politically unfashionable, and Clinton was already a central player in a very different sort of politics. In the 1980s and '90s the Republican war on blacks, the poor, and the already-stingy American welfare state escalated, tapping into long-standing white racist and anti-government resentments. In response, the Democratic Leadership Council (DLC)—a centrist group that sought to rebrand the Democratic Party—whittled away what little resolve Democrats had to defend welfare state programs, allowing the dominant political discourse to become increasingly hostile to the poor.

In 1992, Bill Clinton, actively allied with the DLC, campaigned for the presidency with the promise to "end welfare as we know it," proposing a policy of "two years and off to work." One of Clinton's first initiatives was to make work more rewarding by expanding the earned income tax credit, a federal program dating back to 1975 that supplemented the earnings of low wage workers. These initiatives pulled many low-income households above the poverty line.

However, after the Republicans gained control of the House of Representatives in the 1994 midterm election, the Clintons' approach to the issue changed. The newly elected House, under the leadership of Newt Gingrich, produced a series of bills to eliminate Aid to Families with Dependent Children (AFDC), which had been the main cash assistance program to the poor, its benefits going mostly to women and children. In the days of the "War on Poverty," expanding access to the AFDC rolls was one of the main ways to direct resources into low-income communities. Federal courts recognized the right of eligible households to AFDC assistance, and activists used court rulings to force local officials to provide benefits that had been denied.

The Republican plan was to eliminate this form of federal redress by abolishing AFDC and turning the new program over to the states, giving them wide latitude to deny benefits. It was central to the effort to deny potential recipients the ability to sue in federal courts. Twice the Republicans sent legislation along these lines to President Clinton, who vetoed the legislation as too harsh. Within the White House, there was plenty of disagreement. Hillary Clinton advocated passing the punitive legislation and ending welfare, even as others in the administration, like Labor Secretary Robert Reich and Treasury Secretary Robert Rubin, objected.[3] In August 1996, as President Clinton's reelection campaign loomed, he took Hillary's advice and signed the third bill. This version was called the Personal Responsibility and Work Opportunity Reconciliation Act and it created Temporary Assistance for Needy Families (TANF) to replace AFDC.

Republicans and many Democrats argued for the new program by claiming that government checks to the poor created a condition called "dependency" that sapped recipients of the drive and self-reliance required for economic success. Hardly anyone probed deeply enough to recognize that dependency is part of the human condition.[4] But the plan was that newly trained welfare workers would combat dependency by tough love; they would persuade and, when necessary, coerce, welfare recipients to go out and take jobs. And with states setting strict time limits on a family's welfare eligibility, those who resisted would ultimately be cut off the rolls.[5]

Immediately after its passage, the new legislation was considered a success. The welfare rolls fell rather quickly; so, too, did poverty rates, caused by a booming economy with strong employment growth in the late 1990s. Furthermore, an increase in the minimum wage that was also passed in August 1996, together with the earlier expansion of the earned income tax credit, made jobs at the bottom

of the labor market more rewarding. Many former welfare recipients were able to enter the job market, and some of them were even
able to live above the poverty line.

But these favorable conditions did not last. In 2001, the economy
slid into recession and in the fifteen years since, the labor market
has never again been as tight as it was in 1999. Every indicator
shows that the wages at the bottom of the economy have remained
stagnant. The credits that families with children get from the earned
income tax credit have not been adjusted upwards since 1993, and
the federal minimum wage was only modestly increased in 2009.
So millions of people who previously might have relied on AFDC
are either unable to find employment or have jobs that pay so little
that both rates of poverty and extreme poverty have been climbing.

While the Clinton effort "to make work pay" had a short shelf
life, the TANF legislation endured and it has worked just as its
Republican architects intended. Welfare caseloads have plummeted,
from about 14 million people in 1995 to 4.2 million today. Before
welfare reform, 68 percent of families with children in poverty
received cash assistance. By 2013 it had fallen to 36 percent, and
the assistance these families received was only a fraction of the
poverty line. States receive a TANF block grant from the federal
government, but they are allowed to use that money for other purposes, so they have a strong incentive to deny aid to eligible families
by requiring recipients to look for work first or by simply cutting
them from the rolls for rule infractions. And without recourse to
the courts, there is nothing that the poor or their advocates can do.
It is no surprise then that with millions of people forced into the
labor market, wages and working conditions at the bottom have
deteriorated.

The obstacles to aid are so extreme that during the great recession of 2007 when unemployment exceeded 10 percent—the worst
downturn since the 1930s—sixteen states saw continued declines in
their TANF rolls between 2007 and 2011 even though the number

of unemployed had risen nationally by 71 percent.[6] Since as few as 40 percent of the unemployed are eligible for unemployment insurance in any given month, this meant millions of families were eligible only for food stamps in the midst of a global economic crisis that resulted from the speculative excesses of Wall Street. Because of TANF, the US had effectively regressed to the early 1930s, when many of the unemployed had no recourse other than private charity.

In a word, the Clintons gambled in 1996 that eliminating a legally protected right to assistance for the poor would not, in total, matter because of their policies to improve the compensation of low wage work, such as the higher minimum wage and a larger earned income tax credit. But while the gamble worked in the short term, it ultimately failed because of broad changes in the American labor market.

Had the Clintons been more familiar with the history of welfare policies in England and the US, they might not have made the same mistake. In nineteenth-century England, the principle of "less eligibility" was clearly articulated, and it meant that no prime-age adult receiving assistance should be as well-off as even the lowest paid worker. That principle has in fact shaped programs to assist the poor for centuries, and it helps account for their harshness. It is easy to understand why the employers of low-wage labor insist on less eligibility. Without it, they would have been unable to force people to work in the "dark Satanic mills" of early industrialization. The degradation of the poor that results both from their meager subsistence, and from the ritualized insult that is a condition of receiving that subsistence, has also made them into social pariahs, a despised class, ensuring that most of the time a broader public can be encouraged to turn against them.

The principle of less eligibility has always been cruel to the people who are its victims, and divisive as well since the application of the principle turns those who are barely better off against those who are deemed poor. Indeed, it turns the poor against themselves as they struggle to salvage a bit of dignity in the midst of campaigns of ritualized insult. For example, after the passage of TANF, in the late 1990s welfare recipients in New York City were made to wear bright orange vests as they cleaned the parks. But now the cruelty looms even larger because wage work has become ever more precarious and relegates so many to poverty. If we continue to be obsessed with worries about dependency, we will not be able to solve the problem of poverty as it unfolds in the economy.

Much of the left in the US holds on to its faith in full employment as the panacea that will heal American social problems, including poverty. As one example, Bernie Sanders's presidential campaign focuses on creating full employment, which has been the left's main anti-poverty program for almost a century. On this platform, not only will there be "jobs for all," but tight labor markets will lead to wage increases, stronger unions, and all the social goods that will follow from more powerful unions, including regulation of business, an enlarged commons, and better protections for those who cannot participate in the full employment economy. Some proponents even claim that through the simple expedient of passing legislation to make the federal government "the employer of last resort," permanent full employment will be realized.

Yet the full employment approach to poverty has consistently failed, with terrible consequences for many millions of people left behind. The cautionary tale of the Personal Responsibility and Work Opportunity Reconciliation Act suggests how risky this approach is. We certainly recognize that really tight labor markets can do amazing things as during World War II when long-impoverished people, including Southern black men and women, became skilled shipyard workers earning decent wages, but the real lesson of history is that labor markets have rarely ever been that tight. The reason is obvious. Employers—both large and small—have always mobilized ferociously against a policy of full employment, as they mobilized to defeat the 1945 Full Employment Bill, and did so at the height of organized labor's political power.[7] They have many other tricks in their repertoire, including recruiting workers from beyond the borders of the US. Barring a political upheaval that few of us can imagine, the idea that such employer opposition can be overcome for extended periods of time is little more than a fantasy.

This issue of employer resistance is critical because it is only when labor markets are very tight, as they were briefly in the late 1990s, that one sees real improvements through the labor market for those in poverty. Even today, with unemployment down to around 5 percent, wage levels at the bottom of the labor market are still stagnant and many people have simply given up looking for work. In fact, the labor force participation rate for adults is at its lowest level since the 1970s, and little progress is being made to reduce the number of people who are poor. And yet already mainstream economists are worrying that any further tightening of the labor market would be likely to produce dangerously high rates of inflation.

Trying to achieve full employment is a flawed political and economic strategy for the following compelling reasons:

1. Over the last thirty years, the US has seen a dramatic drop in the manufacturing labor force as a consequence of technological progress and the movement of production overseas. While some manufacturing jobs are coming back, the average new factory employs just a small fraction of the numbers that staffed auto plants a generation ago. Even if one reads skeptically the claims that millions of white collar and service jobs are about to be destroyed by sophisticated robots and thinking machines, it is still likely that existing jobs will disappear faster than new jobs can be created.

2. Economic stagnation and climate change in the Global South have already created an enormous wave of refugees and migrants

seeking safety and opportunity in North America, Europe, and Australia, and there is every reason to believe that this global migration will grow much larger. While Republican presidential candidate Donald Trump and his nativist supporters dream of a wall to keep these people out, simple decency requires that the US and other wealthy countries increase the numbers that are taken in. But an increase in the number of immigrants, with or without documents, will mean even more people fighting for jobs that will continue to be scarce.

3. Even if it were achieved, full employment does not actually solve the complicated tasks of juggling work and family obligations that are so pressing for people today. Often what people need is not more employment, but paid leave to care for children or dying parents or medical crises. And many people want and need part-time jobs that are well compensated and have good benefits because they are combining work and schooling with child-rearing. Those who are in low-wage service sector jobs often complain, more than anything, about the unpredictability of their work schedules. Some of them would gladly work fewer hours in exchange for greater control over their work schedule.

4. Full employment, especially full employment at decent wages, has always been yoked to the imperative of economic growth. But it is now obvious that our historic patterns of resource-intensive economic growth are a threat to the future of the planet. Given the urgent need to respond to global climate change, full employment rhetoric risks playing into the hands of the reactionary forces who insist we must continue burning fossil fuels whatever the cost.

5. Full employment was not always the main credo of the left. In the early nineteenth century, the drudgery and toil, the clocks and whistles of tightly regulated factory work, were resisted by the artisans and farmers who were herded into the spreading

factory system. The early movements for reduced hours, the campaigns first for the ten-hour day, then for the eight-hour day, reflected that resistance. So did the aborted American labor protests against "wage slavery" that followed the passage of the Thirteenth Amendment.

The idea that human freedom meant liberation from work was also at the core of Marx's critique of wage labor and inspired many critical intellectuals. John Maynard Keynes speculated in 1930 that Western nations were on the verge of a general prosperity sufficient to enable the masses of the population to limit their work time to perhaps three hours a day so they could devote the remainder of their time to the enjoyment of art, love, the quest for knowledge, and so on. But nothing like this happened. Although market societies did become steadily richer, there were no further reductions in average working hours after the eight-hour day had become the norm, except in a few affluent European countries.[8] Instead, the demands of work have become ever more insistent, even as many of us accumulate far more things than we actually need or that the planet can sustainably provide.

So what then should be done? We think it is high time to liberate a left policy catechism from its obsession with full employment and the corollary fear of creating "dependency" through government income support. We need to attack problems of poverty directly rather than wait for some glorious future day when full employment will finally arrive. This means that we have to give money and other forms of assistance to the people who need it. We need to return to the idea that was last seriously considered in the late 1960s of creating a guaranteed minimum income for all citizens. This idea has gained increasing support in recent years, including from prominent economists such as Robert Reich, Joseph Stiglitz, and Anthony Atkinson.[9] This approach would simultaneously make a huge dent in poverty, tighten the labor market, and begin to redress the obscene inequality in the distribution of income.

Given the recent hegemony of austerity and government cutbacks, talk of income guarantees may seem like pie in the sky; so too does full employment. Still, if we look beyond the family of Western welfare states, there are actually new models that we might begin to emulate. In direct contradiction to our expectation that the West must lead the way, middle-income countries across the globe have been pioneering cash assistance programs that do not require a record of steady employment by the recipient, as social insurance does. Neither are they conditional on work or make-work regimens, as TANF is. In Latin America, East Asia, and Africa, governments have introduced cash transfer programs that reach huge swaths of the population and are not contorted by the dictums of less eligibility. These make a significant dent in income inequality.[10]

In Brazil, the Bolsa Familia program, which began as an effort to reward poor families for keeping their children in school, now covers one quarter of the population and provides 51 percent of their income. In Mexico, Prospera Programme covers 23.2 million people and contributes 45 percent of their income. Across the globe, 118 countries have instituted broad cash transfer programs.[11] Although the programs are relatively new, they have already had a demonstrable impact on poverty and inequality. A 2012 UN report showed that poverty rates in Latin America had dropped to their lowest level in two decades, from 48.4 percent to 31.4 percent, while the rate of extreme poverty fell from 22.6 percent to 12.3 percent.[12]

Moreover, the boost in public spending was accompanied by an increase in wage income. If anything, these programs seem to prove that giving the poor money does not make them lazy and dependent; on the contrary, protecting them from hunger and homelessness helps them to be more productive.[13] It is just possible that these efforts could be the first steps toward institutionalizing a global basic income established through international cooperation as a strategy to fight both poverty and the devastating consequences of climate change.

We have even seen some small signs of parallel developments in the United States. The Obama administration has pushed an initiative to eliminate homelessness among veterans by providing them with "housing first," which represents a sharp break with earlier policies that insisted on behavior changes before assistance. Cities including Phoenix, Houston, New Orleans, and Salt Lake City have announced success in providing a home for every veteran living on the street. Moreover, the strategy has been cost-effective and has proven better than previous strategies in helping this population deal with the psychiatric and addiction issues that often precede homelessness.

To be sure, the successes of this program come from combining resources from the Veterans Administration with public and private funds raised at the local level. But the point is that social problems *can* be solved by throwing money at them, contrary to the rhetoric of dependency. We could handle the problem of civilian homelessness in the same way. The obstacle is not dependency; it is a lack of political will to spend the money and build more public housing units.

And no one should be allowed to claim that our refusal to spend money to assist those in poverty makes any economic sense. Think of the nearly 3 million children growing up in families in extreme poverty living on $2.00 per person per day or less. Most of these families are homeless or transitory, moving from one tenuous living situation to another. Adequate nutrition for these children is uncertain, and their schooling is regularly disrupted by constant family crises. Household instability means that only a very small fraction of these children will end up graduating from high school, much less college. The irony, of course, is that a substantial percentage of these children will grow up being dependent because of mental problems, addiction, or incarceration. Just as with the homeless vets, it is much better social policy to spend money now on prevention than to deal with ever more costly issues for an entire lifetime.

Our point is that the persistence and deepening of American poverty, the trends in labor markets, and the clear ecological dangers of unceasing economic growth all argue for an entirely different welfare state, one that is unshackled from labor market imperatives. This is unlikely to be accomplished all at once, but we can still keep the grim lessons of less eligibility in mind as we work to move toward a society in which all are ultimately afforded protection from economic hardship. An authentic feminist movement must keep that principle firmly in mind.

THREE

Free the Children!

Amber A'Lee Frost

Hillary Clinton's political biography has all the makings of a neoliberal folktale. A precocious young thing, she cut her electoral teeth canvassing for Nixon in Chicago at the tender age of thirteen. According to Jeff Gerth and Don Van Natta Jr.'s 2007 Pulitzer Prize–winning biography *Her Way: The Hopes and Ambitions of Hillary Rodham Clinton*, young Hillary was incensed by her social studies teacher's tale of assault at the hands of Democratic Party poll watchers. Not only did the spirited eighth-grade Republican use her lunch period to call Mayor Daley and complain, she and a friend joined a group of ambitious Nixonian muckrakers that following Sunday, *without* parental permission, no less. In what must have been a thrilling moment of youthful righteousness, Hillary found that an address listed by dozens of voters was actually a vacant lot. Her joy was cut short when she returned home to a furious father, who, despite his own Cold War anti-communism, was not at all pleased that his adolescent daughter had been knocking on doors in the rough South Side of Chicago. Regardless, it's a compelling story of political awakening, and a fascinating, and ironic, indoctrination for a woman who would eventually be plagued by her own legal and ethics scandals.

In high school, Hillary volunteered for Barry Goldwater's 1964 presidential bid. Goldwater was a virulently anti-communist candidate, considered far too right-wing for mainstream Republicans in his economic conservatism. According to her autobiography, Hillary read Goldwater's landmark polemic, *Conscience of a Conservative*, in ninth grade and was attracted to him as a "rugged individualist"— she wore a cowgirl outfit and a straw hat along with her "AuH2O" pin, again foreshadowing the bubba-drawl she would later adopt on the more rustic paths of the campaign trail.

Predictably, college brought with it some ideological revisions, but while her work on Eugene McCarthy's campaign insinuates some anti-war sympathies, she also interned for Gerald Ford when he was Republican leader of the House, and she worked on then New York governor Nelson Rockefeller's bid for the GOP presidential nomination. It wasn't until Yale Law, when she took part in the investigation of Nixon (again, another interesting note on corruption, especially given that Bob Woodward himself has drawn parallels between her email scandals and the troubles of the Nixon White House) and when she worked with Bill on George McGovern's campaign, that she made the switch to Democrat.

Clinton's move to the Dems was the opening gambit of a career-long strategy for political success—hitching her wagon to a winning horse (in this case, Bill). While her political "flexibility" has mostly been conventional, Clinton was in her youth not entirely unreceptive to radical thought. In fact, the right-wingers who sought to portray her as a ball-busting feminist once focused on the area in which her addressed gender politics have been most complex: motherhood and the home.

By far the most fascinating and peculiar aspect of Hillary's political development was her engagement with children's rights, a movement during her law school days that was actually led by both civil rights leaders and the left-most feminists of the second wave, a movement that was an extension of the first wave and women's social reformers. Now that children were out of the sweatshops, radical feminists such as Shulamith Firestone fought for an even more liberated child, as in her groundbreaking 1970 book, *The Dialectic of Sex: The Case for Feminist Revolution.* With all of Firestone's impassioned calls to feminist revolution, and the fascinating future she prescribes for a postgender world (robotic wombs to replace pregnancy is the one that usually gets the most press), her radical child advocacy has been overlooked. Chapter 4, "Down with Childhood," sets the tone for the second wave's "wild" ideas about kids. Like many of her feminist peers—and many who came before her—Firestone believed that the welfare of women and that of children were fundamentally interconnected. She believed both that the nature of the bond between mother and child is "no more than shared oppression"[1] and that "the best way to raise a child is to LAY OFF!"[2]

While Hillary's foray into children's rights was tamer (and it's unlikely that she owned a dog-eared copy of *The Dialectic of Sex*), her early work for children's rights reflected the radical ideas of this period. Her first job out of law school was with the Children's Defense Fund, a nonprofit children's advocacy group primarily founded in the context of civil rights in 1973, the same year Hillary published an article titled "Children Under the Law," which would become infamous.[3] That and her 1977 essay "Children's Rights: A Legal Perspective" were most certainly the result of the ideological atmosphere created by such radical minds as Firestone.[4]

During Bill's campaign for the presidency, the work came back to haunt her. By this time, she was an abstinence-education-touting, junk-food-hating, violence-on-television-fearing mom, yet she was perceived by many conservatives as a fascinatingly radical feminist, someone Firestone would certainly have preferred to the real 1990s Hillary's convoluted lanyard of kiddie liberation and nanny-state protectionism. In a 1992 speech, Chairman of the Republican National Committee Richard N. Bond said that Hillary "likened marriage and the family to slavery. She has referred to the family as a dependency relationship that deprives people of their rights."[5]

Ironically, this Republican hit job was 100 percent true. In "Children Under the Law," she wrote, "The basic rationale for depriving people of rights in a dependency relationship is that certain individuals are incapable or undeserving of the right to take care of themselves ... Along with the family, past and present examples of such arrangements include marriage, slavery and the Indian reservation system."[6]

Compare this to her 1990 editorial in the *New York Times*:

> Throughout the 1980's, debate over child care in the U.S. always seemed to focus on "family values." This assumes that parents alone can always determine and then provide—personally or through the marketplace—what's best for their children and, hence, society.
>
> But this view has allowed our Government and, to a much larger extent, business to ignore the needs of America's children and their parents. It also discounts the extent to which economic realities determine access to quality child care.[7]

She hedges, of course, and mentions earlier on that "given the differences in political philosophies and tax structures between our nations we should not duplicate the French system here—wholesale," but there is a glimmer of her law school self, with just enough vagueness to allow wiggle-room for Bill's "end of welfare as we know it."

The fight for children's welfare is Hillary's only claim to a legitimately leftist political history and certainly her only claim to anything close to the deep end of the feminist pool. Every bit of that is eviscerated entirely by her policy-making record.

After Bill passed welfare reform as president, with Hillary's exhortation and encouragement, the Children's Defense Fund denounced the Clintons openly, with founder Marian Wright Edelman saying that Bill Clinton's "signature on this pernicious bill makes a mockery of his pledge not to hurt children."[8] Oddly Edelman's position softened over the years; in 2007 she said, "Hillary Clinton is an old friend, but [the Clintons] are not friends in politics."[9] By 2013, however, Edelman was positively glowing in a press release:

> CDF is pleased to recognize Hillary Rodham Clinton, who has been a tireless voice for children. She's brilliant. She cares deeply about children. She perseveres. She's an incredibly hard worker, and she stays with it. She's done extraordinarily well in everything she's ever done and I'm just so proud of her.[10]

Hillary's single, completely anomalous left-wing predilection for children certainly makes sense on a cultural level; the 1970s were a period of radical change, when issues of feminism, race, and childhood were understood to be tightly connected. As a highly adaptive politician, it made perfect sense for her to reflect the momentum of the times. Children are also, arguably, the *only* feminist or antiracist subjects conservatives are willing to acknowledge as "deserving poor," and advocating for them could be construed (as it later was) as bipartisan. When inconvenient, of course, children can also be ignored. The majority of welfare beneficiaries have always been children, but by 2002, Clinton was so proud of welfare reform that she boasted, "These people are no longer deadbeats, they're actually out there being productive."[11] One can only assume she wasn't referring to kids.

The presumed lead candidate for the Democratic nomination for president of the United States of America would now be completely unrecognizable as a feminist to many feminists of her generation, the famously radical women of the second wave on which Hillary—consciously or not—built her career.

There is no mention of welfare by Hillary's die-hard supporters because, despite the alleged era of "intersectional" feminism, civil rights, poverty, and the welfare of children have been effectively cleaved from feminism. Since the second wave, the mainstream feminist movement abandoned its most radical tendencies and certainly its materialist policy goals. Unlike the movement of the 1970s, there is no mass call beyond representation, and an opportunist like Hillary has no incentive whatsoever to reflect the interests of women in her policies, despite who she claims to represent. The feminist movement has set on an entirely different course since Hillary's law school days, and she has followed suit.

Of course, *no* president of the United States, no matter how well meaning, will end the exploitation of workers, and therefore the exploitation of women, children, and people of color, all by herself. Back in the 1970s, much of the progressive and feminist change—and radical ideas like those that young Hillary wrote about in her law review articles—also emerged out of grassroots political ferment. With any luck, Hillary's use of feminist ideas to endorse bourgeois ends will only convince more people of the importance of efforts such as these.

FOUR

Waging War on Teachers

Megan Erickson

I
f second wave feminists intended to undo illusions about the
existence of separate public and private spheres with the rallying
cry that "the personal is political," Hillary Clinton has spent her
life demonstrating the truth of this slogan.

The deep interconnectedness of the Clintons' public and private
lives, for better and for worse, is a constant, abiding theme even
in the story they tell about themselves, predating the bitchy newspaper columns and mostly petulant witch hunts of congressional
Republicans during Bill's presidency and impeachment trial. It is
now clearer than ever that the Clintons' relationship is a partner-
ship built on the foundation of a unified ideology that serves as a
moral code for both Bill and Hillary. It is impossible to talk about
the political strategy—or, to use today's individualist parlance,
the "vision" and "achievements"—of one Clinton without talking
about the other.

This is particularly true when it comes to matters they care deeply about—and education is unlucky enough to be one of those. "We always considered Bill and Hillary as one working unit," Sidney Johnson, president of the Arkansas Education Association during Bill's governorship, told the *New York Times* on the eve of Clinton's first presidential inauguration. "Something would come down and you wouldn't know which of them thought of it, where Bill stopped and Hillary began. That's why we called them Billary."[1]

Billary was also an early and influential backer of corporate education reforms—more intensely than is commonly understood today, either by charter school advocates or teachers' union activists.[2] The "something" to which Johnson referred was a sweeping set of changes to the state's schools, initiated after a lower court determined that the gross disparities in funding between rich and poor districts (which characterized Arkansas's system of financing public education) were discriminatory. "During Clinton's upcoming term, it was virtually certain that the Supreme Court would uphold the lower court and toss the matter back at the governor and the legislature to solve. Better that Clinton get in front of the issue and use the case to his advantage," Hillary's biographer, Carl Bernstein, writes.[3]

In 1983, then governor Clinton nominated the first lady to chair a task force that would meet seventy-five times in three months and single-handedly determine the agenda for education reform in the state. As he observed rather sweetly, "This guarantees that I will have a person who is closer to me than anyone else overseeing a project that is more important to me than anything else."[4] The heart of the proposed reform package was the introduction of statewide standardized tests for students as well as a competence test for teachers, funded by a 1 percent increase in the state sales tax— the burden of which fell flatly and equally on rich and poor and is obviously more consequential to the latter. This, in a state that is home to some of the largest corporations in the country, including Tyson Foods, the Stephens Corporation, and Walmart, all of which

Governor Clinton "went to bat for" more than once, "doing all he could to promote industrial development."[5] Hillary Clinton would later sit on the board of directors of Walmart from 1986 to 1992 and receive $20,000 in donations from the Walmart political action committee during her 2008 campaign. She was close to the Walton family (the heirs to Sam Walton, founder of Walmart), who would become nationally influential players in the corporate education reform movement.

Founded in the late 1980s, the Walton Family Foundation first started putting money into charter schools in the early to mid 1990s. Her seat on the Walmart board was designed especially for her (she was not filling an open seat), and she held $100,000 in stock (at a time when Bill was making $35,000 a year). Walmart Foundation has since donated millions of dollars to the Clinton Foundation.

Needing a scapegoat for poor school performance, it was the Arkansas State Teachers Association the Clintons chose to vilify, a tactic that would come to characterize corporate education reform throughout the 1990s—just like the broader tactic of shifting from discussion of social and political inequities in funding to talk of standards and accountability for individuals. From Bernstein, again:

> "[Hillary] made it very clear that there had to be a bad guy in this," said Richard Herget, Bill's campaign chairman. "Anytime you're going to turn an institution upside down, there's going to be a good guy and a bad guy. The Clintons painted themselves as the good guys. The bad guys were the schoolteachers." The day before Hillary's plan was announced publicly, Bill told the head of the Arkansas Education Association [Sidney Johnson] that teacher-testing would be part of the reform package. The official was, predictably, furious.[6]

Hillary justified her insistence on the competency test by claiming that when attending public hearings, and traveling to every Arkansas district, she "kept hearing stories about grossly incompetent teachers who could hardly read or spell."[7] Perhaps even more saliently, Dick Morris's polling had found that 50 percent of voters would support a tax increase to fund education, but 85 percent would support it if teacher testing were part of the reforms.

If Arkansans were going to be compelled to fund public education for children, they were determined to do so only at the expense of teachers. Never mind that Arkansas teachers were the poorest paid in the country, receiving a salary of only $10,000 a year and living on food stamps in some areas, or that civil rights organizations openly condemned the teacher test provision since it was black teachers who were most likely to lose their jobs as a result. Of the many infractions against meaning and language committed by contemporary education reformers, the most insidious has been the apparent transformation of the words "standards" and "accountability" into a matter of apolitical bookkeeping.

But this was not just cynical maneuvering on the part of the Clintons—it was and is fully in line with their principles. Hillary Clinton believed and continues to believe, along with corporate education reformers, that the biggest crisis faced in America, and in its schools, is a crisis of values, not a crisis of inequity. "The first purpose of school is to educate," she argued then, "not to provide entertainment or opportunities to socialize. Discipline holds no mystery. When it is firm, clearly understood, fairly administered and perceived to be so, it works. When it doesn't, it doesn't."[8] A decade later, during the 1992 presidential campaign, she would tell an audience of rapt New York City eighth graders that schools should assign more homework. In 2015, she proclaimed, "I believe it is time we get back to teaching discipline, self-control, patience, punctuality. The biggest complaint that I hear from employers is that young people who show up for jobs don't have those habits.

They don't get there on time. They don't know how to conduct themselves appropriately."⁹

Of course, it's obvious that this is part of what drew Bill to Hillary in the first place. Even in her bespectacled "leftish" phase, before she lost the crimped hair, bell-bottoms and "hippie" feminism, she was careful. When she was still in law school at Yale, an organized May Day "uprising" ended with someone setting fire to the International Law Library. It was Hillary who rushed in with the bucket brigade and took it upon herself to walk a beat as a member of the security patrol "protecting the university's resources and property," according to her biographer Carl Bernstein.¹⁰

In an almost bizarrely earnest 1993 interview with Michael Kelly, the Washington correspondent for the *New York Times*, titled (with some skepticism, as well as admiration) "Saint Hillary," Clinton muses, "The very core of what I believe is this concept of individual worth, which I think flows from all of us being creatures of God and being imbued with a spirit." At another point, much later in the piece, she rejects rights-based liberalism, asserts that she favors welfare reform, and, doing her best impression of a Midwestern mom, "argues that society has extended too freely rights without responsibilities, which has led to a great decline in the standard of behavior." She says, "Senator Moynihan argues very convincingly that what we have in effect done is get used to more and more deviant behavior around us, because we haven't wanted to deal with it. But—by gosh!—it is deviant! It is deviant if you have any standards by which you expect to be judged."

This conservatism is particularly evident when we look at her influence on education policy.

Back in Arkansas, Hillary presented her reform program to the state legislature in a five-week special session. It was adopted in its entirety. It was Clinton's first attempt, according to Dick Morris, "to merge Democratic compassion with the Republican notion of responsibility,"¹¹ and perhaps also the first example of Hillary playing the public policy version of "bad cop" to uphold Bill's good guy appearances. As early as 1992, the program was widely regarded as more of a political stunt than an enduring transformation to the state education system. But it did get the Clintons noticed.

In 1989, Bill and Hillary travelled to the seminal Charlottesville Education Summit convened by then president George H. W. Bush. No educators were invited, but there were plenty of business leaders present, along with Dick and Lynne Cheney. Christopher T. Cross, who was at the time working for the Republican Department of Education, recalls that Bush "went out of his way at several points during the closing remarks to acknowledge [Bill] Clinton's work."[12]

One of the major results of the summit, says Cross, was a consensus to set national performance goals in education—an unprecedented move for the party of states' rights and local control. The political tradeoff was that the goals focused on educational outcomes (test scores) rather than inputs (textbooks, teacher salaries, student/teacher ratio, and so on). The Cheneys felt that "the education community had remained preoccupied with issues like the number of books, the number of students per teacher, the dollars available for this, the number of that, while failing to look at what the educational system was producing: are students learning a year's worth of education for every year of teaching? … Do graduates have the academic skills they need to succeed in a job or in college?"[13]

This consciously organized shift in reform emphasis had nothing to do with research, which has found repeatedly that money matters very much in educational outcomes.[14] Instead, it had everything to do with the corporate agenda that was embraced by many Democratic and Republican politicians even as early as the 1990s. (H. W. Bush was the first Republican with the ambition to be an "education president," for example, and No Child Left Behind was a strikingly bipartisan piece of legislation.) Corporate interests wishing to reduce government spending increasingly balked at the cost of K-12 education, an irksome and intractable entitlement in a society with few universal government benefits. It's essential to understand that while spending on American schools in the past four decades has in fact doubled (a figure trumpeted by corporate reformers hell-bent on making the case for depriving schools of additional funding), more than half of the increase has gone toward special education, as Americans have arrived at the conclusion that children with special needs have a right to a public education in the least restrictive environment possible, rather than institutionalization.[15]

Reformers who emphasize standardized testing and teacher accountability over inputs/money often claim to do so because of concerns over young people's presumed lack of preparation for high tech jobs. Hillary Clinton was a pioneer of this line of argument, serving as a member of the W. T. Grant Foundation Commission on Youth and America's Future, which published a report in 1988 on the need to improve occupational training for non-college-bound youth.

But the truth is, these jobs don't exist—the greatest area of growth in the job market for years to come was then, and still is projected to be, in the often low-paying service sector. The "skills gap" is a myth. The commitment of corporate education reformers to teacher accountability as a proxy for correcting long-standing injustices in the distribution of resources is a rhetorical gesture to justify "punishing" students, schools, and teachers with ever-escalating austerity and disciplinary measures. Forcing teachers and students to produce results is not about improving education or making it more equitable; it is about controlling current and future workers—teachers, a group of unionized public sector workers of significant social capital, and, of course, children, who make up the workforce of the future.

There was absolute continuity between the Clintons' Arkansas agenda and their plans for the nation's schools once they attained the White House. A package of national standards reminiscent of the Arkansas program, Goals 2000, was the first legislative proposal set forth by the Clinton presidential administration, signifying their intent to repeat the strategies that worked for them in Arkansas. Asked whether Hillary would play a role in education policy in his presidency, Clinton said, "She knows a lot more than I do about some of this stuff."[16]

In Clintonian political discourse, emphasis on getting things done—*productivity*—and who's doing them—*representation*—replaces interrogation into what is being accomplished, and how; who wins and who loses; which women and which children.

On August 30, 2015, Hillary's official Twitter account highlighted a "big question from a small supporter in Iowa: How will Hillary get things done?" In a forty-second video, a charmingly articulate little girl asks Hillary how she will deliver on her campaign promises when Republicans have a majority in congress. Her (respectful) response: "If you say what you're going to do and you keep saying it over and over and over again, you can get more people to expect it and get more cooperation. I also hope to help more Democrats get elected so it's not quite as lopsided as it is now. The other thing is, like when I was in the Senate or the secretary of state, you just have to work with them all the time and find where are those areas that we can cooperate on? And then you do something." *Doing something* becomes a goal in itself, neatly sidestepping specifics.

In 2016, I will not be casting a vote for the woman who "gets things done." I will not be voting for the Clintons, who have spent their lives together calling for—*and living*—a politics of personal respectability and political compromise and tolerance as a solution to a society that is intolerably segregated by race and class, where *Plessy vs. Ferguson* is the rule and *Brown vs. Board of Ed.* the underwhelming exception. I will not be voting for a leader interested in "the biggest complaint about young people" from employers, and I will certainly not be voting for anyone who advocates for the education of children based on their potential as future workers, rather than the fact that they are alive now, today, and are presently among the most vulnerable and exploited of human beings. We owe them the positive freedom to survive and thrive.

If we have learned anything during this era of unfettered markets and global free trade fiercely supported by the Clintons, it's that the system will not mete out justice piece by piece. When workers strike in the factory, owners will simply move their business to the next city or the next shore. No single personality, however big, whether male or female, can chip away at our rapid and unjust free market capitalism through years of compromise or innovations in political strategy that lead to minor reforms, because the system is not at all fragile but very strong. It is as dynamic, flexible, and international as the very labor force on whose backs it has been built. This is a terrifying truth, but once we accept it, we find new possibilities in the place of the "new politics" of Third Way reform, which despite the best efforts and intentions of foundations like the Clinton Global Initiative, is dead. What we need is a little more of the old politics. What we need is working-class men, women, and children of all colors and ethnicities marching together in the streets. What we need is parents, teachers, and children opting out of a system that is imposed on them, to build their own. What we need is not a woman for president; what we need is a movement.

FIVE

Neoliberal Fictions: Harper Lee, Hillary Clinton and My Dad

Catherine Liu

Just as Hillary Clinton's inevitable campaign for the US presidency was gearing up in the summer of 2015, America was reviving its ongoing celebration of Harper Lee's novel *To Kill a Mockingbird*. The simultaneous veneration of these two cultural icons made sense to me. They have something in common: my father is a huge fan of both.

Otherwise indifferent or condescending about feminism and the women's movement, Dad finds the front-runner for the 2016 Democratic nomination irresistible. In politics, my father reserves his respect for paranoid anti-liberal or even radical types like Richard Nixon and Mao Zedong. Dad enjoys a whiff of authoritarianism; Clinton's demeanor makes the Chinese immigrant feel right at home.

So, too, does Harper Lee's perennial middlebrow best seller. Especially heralded amid controversy over the unlikely publication, fifty-five years later, of an alleged sequel, *Go Set a Watchman*,

Dad would agree with Adam Gopnik and National Public Radio that *To Kill a Mockingbird* is a literary "masterpiece."[1] Dad is of a generation of Chinese American immigrants who are thoughtlessly racist when it comes to black Americans. In 1983, when I was home on spring break from my sophomore year at Yale, Dad and I had fights about race. At twenty, armed with liberal arts–infused arguments and ideas, I thought the first step to "raising his consciousness" was to point out to Dad that he held racist views. He threw a stainless steel plate at me from across the living room and it smashed, Frisbee-like, into my upper arm. I had a bruise for weeks. (Twenty-five years later, I would again find his refusal to vote for Barack Obama racist, but I had by then learned to be a bit more diplomatic.)

Yet during the 1960s, 1970s, and 1980s, Dad himself was the victim of countless racist snubs, or what we would call today microaggressions. In Taiwan, he had been a brilliant young man, full of energy and promise. In New York City, he was a short Asian man with a heavy accent. Even though he succeeded in the US beyond his wildest dreams by landing a job as a translator at the United Nations, negotiating the simplest aspects of American life with Americans of any race has not been easy for him.

Dad likes to protect himself against the vagaries of fate and the casual racism of white America by holding on to the things that make Asian immigrants feel safe: money in the bank, internationally recognizable brands, and winning sports franchises (Vince Lombardi's Green Bay Packers and the 1970s Oakland Raiders). Like most immigrants but also like most Americans, he wants to be reassured that our social order is a fair one. Like *To Kill a Mockingbird*, the narrative of Hillary's ascension to the presidency—America is always getting more inclusive, we just had a black president and now we are getting a woman—is a comforting story in this regard. But such stories not only mask the reality of neoliberalism, they help to sustain it.

Both the novel and the potential first female president represent a purely cosmetic form of diversity that works against the structural changes that need to be made at every level of culture and politics to expose and depose a political class that has acted with impunity to promote policies that benefit wealthy donors and powerful multinational corporations.

To Kill a Mockingbird left a deep imprint upon midcentury readers on the Cold War periphery. To herald the release of *Go Set a Watchman*, the manuscript discovered by Harper Lee and published by Rupert Murdoch–owned HarperCollins, a chapter was excerpted in Murdoch's *Wall Street Journal* as a "teaser" (giving us all a lesson in vertically integrated, transmedia marketing). At this point in history, the reception of *To Kill a Mockingbird* is so well coordinated that Rupert Murdoch's media empire did not need to do much to wring profits from the sales of a sequel with an initial 2-million-copy print run. *Watchman's* reviewers worried about how *Mockingbird's* fans were going to react when they discovered that Atticus Finch was an unrepentant racist. Otherwise cold-blooded professionals like Michiko Kakutani of the *New York Times* fretted in print about the disappointment that Lee's "fans" would experience after discovering that Atticus was not Gregory Peck, or worse, that he was a defender of Jim Crow, racism, states' rights and segregation.[2] Moreover, *Watchman* captures the casual talk of a small town Southern elite, parroting Father Coughlin–inspired conspiracy theories comparing communists, Catholics, and rebellious blacks, fomenting rebellion.

While the provenance of *Go Set a Watchman* is clouded by scandal, *To Kill a Mockingbird's* purity and quality are unquestioned.[3] When the novel turned fifty in 2010, Oprah Winfrey tried desperately to get an interview with Harper Lee for her show, gushing that *Mockingbird* was our "national novel."[4] Lee was unmoved and refused to be interviewed. The *New York Times* was not happy about the Rupert Murdoch empire publishing the "pseudo-event" of

Watchman. While he condemned HarperCollins's exploitation of an old woman's powerful brand, columnist Joe Nocera described *To Kill a Mockingbird* as a "gem."[5]

My father's relationship to Lee's novel is an especially personal one. In the early 1960s, he was commissioned by a Taiwanese daily to translate a serialized version of Lee's Pulitzer Prize–winning book. Of this achievement, he is extremely proud. The Cold War moral capital of the novel endowed its Chinese translator with an aura of American power and legitimacy. Three years after he finished the serialized translation, he was on his way to the United States.

As a college activist in the 1970s, I did not share my dad's pride in this novel. *To Kill a Mockingbird* was an embarrassment to young people: a relic of the pre–civil rights era whose theater of anti-racism was designed to show how good Southern whites could be. African Americans were making their own history and culture, whereas *To Kill a Mockingbird* spread the news that white Americans were more enlightened and modern than the stories about the Jim Crow South would suggest.[6] To my dad, it must have suggested that a basic goodness and fairness filled the hearts of ordinary white Americans. The image of Atticus as played by tall, gentle and WASPy Gregory Peck was seared into my mind for life: here was the ideal Cold War father. Like a refugee from my own self-hatred, I fled from my father's admiration of Lee's fictional world. But the counterculture critique of the book did not stick; today Lee's novel seems to be more celebrated than ever and has become required reading in the Common Core curriculum for fourteen to fifteen year olds across the United States.

For Lee's dramatization of Jim Crow Southern life and its villains and heroes, she received a Pulitzer Prize, a National Medal of Freedom (from President George W. Bush), and a National Medal of Arts (from President Barack Obama). My father's admiration for Hillary Clinton, however, is even more visceral. He kept a signed eight-by-ten-inch portrait of her that she "sent" him in 2008 after he contributed to her campaign. Well into his eighties, sharp of mind and impervious to arguments about gender equality, my immigrant father is devoted to Hillary.

My father admired the Clintons for their ambition and ruthlessness. Yes, there were the scandals, but that was just part of the game. Hillary Clinton was on a relentless quest for power, like Henry Kissinger; she complained, like Richard Nixon, about being persecuted by implacable enemies. Unlike their conservative adversaries fighting communism and the cultural revolution of the 1960s and 1970s, the Clintons seemed to augur a post-ideological age—but of course it was only post-ideological in the sense that since capitalism had won, there was no other ideology around to compete.

In his critique of the inadequacy of anti-racism, Adolph Reed writes:

> as the basis for a politics, antiracism seems to reflect, several generations downstream, the victory of the postwar psychologists in depoliticizing the critique of racial injustice by shifting its focus from the social structures that generate and reproduce racial inequality to an ultimately individual, and ahistorical, domain of "prejudice" or "intolerance."[7]

Lee's novel argues that meaningful political activity is achieved because Scout and her brother Jem *see* the racism and prejudice of their hometown: anti-racism becomes a series of cognitive exercises in self-improvement. *To Kill a Mockingbird* reinforces the liberal fantasy that anti-racism is about good white people defending helpless black people. It created an image of American goodness that was a powerful Cold War cultural tool for winning hearts and minds.

Bill Clinton's New Democrats promoted the values of neoliberal anti-racism by playing on the "politics" of representation and visibility, ignoring structural contradictions in favor of struggles over self-cultivation, self-control, and self-esteem. During Clinton's presidency, "multiculturalism" and "diversity" were cosmetic concepts, strategically promoted by liberal institutions. The Clintons vacationed and played golf with rich black Americans on Martha's Vineyard, while the president destroyed welfare and dismantled the Glass-Steagall Act that limited commercial banking activities.

American exceptionalism is founded on the idea of meritocracy, a social order that rewards the truly talented and innovative. While "meritocracy" was a satirical term used by British socialist Michael Young to describe postwar oligarchies, overseers of the neoliberal order like Bill Clinton and Tony Blair celebrated it. Like Obama, Hillary Clinton is one of the meritocracy's golden children.[8] Under meritocratic rule, American exceptionalism tells us that we do not need systems of social welfare because we are a nation uniquely capable of leveling all playing fields and creating equality of opportunity for an astounding array of people of all races, sexualities, and, more recently, all gender identifications. American institutions are meant to reward intelligence and hard work and punish stupidity and idleness. That the Clintons are building dynastic forms of power and wealth linking private foundations, shadowy nonprofits, billionaires' fortunes, and young bright ambitious people willing to take on the unvetted agendas of Eli Broad or Bill Gates does not, it would seem, discredit the myth of the meritocracy.

The 2008 financial crisis shook our faith in the unique combination of social triage and free market capitalism: but memories are short and presidential campaigns are long. Bill Clinton and the Democratic Party that he reshaped did not simply deregulate financial institutions and slash federally funded programs for the poor: he also prepared the ground for the growth of a new oligarchy. Clinton may try to defend the repeal of Glass-Steagall, but most economic historians agree that the rampant speculation and profit taking it enabled directly drove widespread financial malfeasance that has still largely gone unpunished.[9] Bill Clinton was able to combine post-1968 institutionalized cultural identity politics with fervor for fiscal policies that made the wealthiest Democratic Party donors as happy as their Republican counterparts.

Economic polarization among every group of Americans is increasing while economic segregation defines urban and suburban growth.[10] Jennifer Silva's study *Coming Up Short: Working Class Adulthood in an Age of Uncertainty* is a poignant examination of the lives of young working-class adults in the face of enormous economic and cultural adversity. Silva found that working-class people of all races and genders struggle to achieve the stability necessary for building meaningful relationships, much less establish families. Often one paycheck away from homelessness or destitution, they seek solace in the hyperindividualistic language of self-help, trying to adjust to difficult and even impossible situations by focusing on positive visualizations or self-esteem. When they fall short of the social and economic expectations that define adulthood and individualization, they tend to blame themselves.[11] Rather than addressing economic and political policies that have relegated 47.5 million Americans to lives of material and psychic deprivation, Democrats and Republicans alike have seized upon punishing regimes of assessment and educational measurement in order to train the imaginary "workforces of the future."

Hillary's political strategy in the Senate was to do as little as possible while courting Republican allies.[12] A Cosimo de' Medici–like strategy of remaining inscrutable and passive while amassing great fortune and political power has its appeal. The pure political inertia whereby inevitability reproduces itself as inevitability might work, but let us have clear eyes about what Hillary Clinton represents—an authoritarian neoliberal status quo. There is nothing revolutionary in her trajectory, despite all claims to the contrary.

Hillary Clinton's platform expropriates the political power of feminism to promote her presidential candidacy as the realization of more than a century of political struggle for women's rights. What does Hillary Clinton's political progress tell us about contemporary politics in the United States? We cannot understand her presidential race and possible presidency without understanding how she and her husband have been able to consolidate a powerful strain of neoliberal ideology. They have successfully reframed the political project of the Democratic Party as a series of highly rationalized, new media- and new technology-friendly protocols of "personal responsibility," self-improvement, assessment and, failing those, punishment. Bill Clinton promised to end welfare as we knew it. He did so with alacrity and in the spirit of building a new brand for the Democratic Party. Seen as being soft on poverty and in favor of soul-sapping big government, Democrats had suffered under the endless reiterations of fake bootstrapping promoted by Ronald Reagan against anything that smacked of socialism or safety nets. In 1996, after years of Republican demonization of the poor, Clinton increased his political capital by showing that Democrats could be equally vicious to the most economically marginalized and exploited.[13]

Feminism taught us that political progress would be achieved when large numbers of women entered political life and achieved professional success and visibility. We have Hillary Clinton. Anti-racism demanded that white people work on their prejudices. We have Atticus Finch and his daughter Scout. All have shady dimensions—Hillary has scandals, the Finches are revealed as crudely racist—but these disappointments are a distraction. Even if they were as inspiring as we wanted them to be, these comforting icons could not lighten the real burdens breaking the backs of the majority of working people in this country.

Economic issues must be front and center again for any movement that really wants to change the way politics and economics are organized. Race and gender inequality are entrenched in unjust economic policies that punish the poor. Gallup polls have shown that the majority of people of color prioritize economic issues as an area of concern—a "concern" that can be mobilized to have greater social impact than campus-based "diversity" initiatives.[14] Class war will always be a real threat in a country where economic polarization policies enrich the few while immiserating the many. A vote for Hillary Clinton will not be a vote for any kind of progress: the Clintons are of the Old Regime, sharing private jets with billionaires and centa-millionaires and using the suffering of others to prop up their monstrous foundation.

To Dad, Hillary represents steely determination, survival and realpolitik. Dad doesn't want Hillary humanized or softened, he likes her just the way she is: a consummate political survivor bent on global domination. He likes the fact that she and her husband have "made the mistakes of the powerful"; he likes the fact that her political brand demands unwavering and unquestioning loyalty. I can imagine that her desire for power and her willingness to point to conspiracies arrayed against her are reminiscent of the political atmosphere of the Cold War world in which he came of age.

But we, the vast majority of Americans, should be angry at the realization of how claims of feminism have been used as tools against us. Very angry. It is time to transform the political culture of this country. Let's reject the latest focus-group-sculpted, hyper-produced political package. The powerful continue to justify their exploitation with everything at their disposal, including the language and platform of equality itself. Perhaps this is the year all that can begin to change.

SIX

The Great Ambivalence

Tressie McMillan Cottom

I want to trust Hillary Clinton more than I do.

My threshold for trusting any politician is low. Currently, the bar is right above "anyone selling wooden nickles" and below "anything for sale on the Home Shopping Network."

I don't exactly trust Barack Obama, but I trusted him about as much as I trusted Bush the elder. I trusted Bush II, the legacy, to be exactly what he was, which is not inspiring, but is a type of trust.

But that's the rub: Hillary isn't some other politician. She has been in the political arena for almost my entire life of political awareness. Her husband was the first president I could vote for. I remember the scandals, the saxophones, and the headbands. My memory of those years may now appear in soft focus but as I recall, the implicit promise was that Bill and Hillary were a twofer. His accomplishments would also be hers because she would be there, in the trenches. Hillary was smart and invested in policy. She chafed at the role of merely decorative first lady. Hillary's record is also Bill's record, and that is not just the narrative of revisionist Republican smear campaigns.

If I cash in the 1990s promise of a Clinton twofer, then I have to consider what that tells me about Hillary, the presidential candidate. While Democrats are running from Obamacare, those of us with the good sense to value public health could credit Hillary for trying it first. Even though the Clintons' push for health care failed miserably (we were then living in the peak of an economic bubble; jobless recoveries were beyond our collective imaginations), I could respect Hillary for setting in motion something I value.

Yet Bill Clinton's post-presidential career raises issues. The Clinton Foundation, an entity in which Hillary has been a full partner, as she has been in all things Bill, has complicated and troubling relationships with sundry corporations, foreign entities (both national and supranational), and universities. Whether this is *normal* is something different from whether it is ethical or acceptable. Take, for instance, for-profit colleges like Strayer University, the University of Phoenix and a hundred other brands you may have seen on television. My own research shows that for-profit colleges make money from social inequalities. There is no shortage of companies in this vein. From check-cashing services for those that banks do not serve, to buy-here-pay-here car lot financing for those who can't qualify for traditional auto financing, there is always a lot of money to be made from selling high-cost services to vulnerable people. For-profit colleges go a bit further. They do not provide a service to vulnerable people so much as they sell a voucher for insurance against social and economic inequalities. And they do this by leveraging our collective faith in education. The large corporate shareholder owners of some of the nation's largest for-profit colleges have extracted billions of public money for private profit. They have primarily done this by manufacturing demand for credentials from those most vulnerable in a labor market where there is little social insurance left for workers. I argue that this works across race, class, and gender—for-profit colleges prey upon shared economic vulnerabilities among their likely students (while leaving too many of these students with more debt than mobility in the long run). But without a doubt, these vulnerabilities are deeper, and the risks greater, for African American women.

That's why the Clinton Foundation's relationship with Laureate International Universities bothers me so much. Between 2010 and 2014, tax returns show that Laureate paid Bill Clinton over $16 million.[1] Those payments were in addition to donations Laureate made to the Clinton Foundation. What does a company like Laureate get for that kind of money? They get an "honorary chancellor" who used to be the leader of one of the most powerful nations in the world. It's a good deal. When you're selling private sector, for-profit education credentials as a kind of quasi social insurance program for the world's vulnerable, leading with Bill Clinton's endorsement has to be a big help. Bill wrote when he stepped down as honorary chancellor in 2015 that "Laureate students represent the next generation of leadership."[2] I have to wonder if he would think highly enough of Laureate to trust them with his own child and grandchildren; since his only child holds degrees from Stanford, Columbia, and Oxford and none from for-profit colleges, we know the answer to this question. In any case, in the 1990s the Clintons described themselves as a political package deal, and there is every reason to think that she is just as implicated in Bill's disturbing relationship with Laureate as she has been in everything Bill has ever done.

To be fair to Hillary, she has uttered some tough campaign rhetoric about for-profit colleges. She says she would crack down on deceptive marketing tactics, like the "pain funnel" wherein some for-profit colleges use a prospective student's deepest fears to "motivate" them to enroll. As far as such things go, Clinton's position is politically expedient. Other candidates like Bernie Sanders have similar positions on for-profit colleges.

Cracking down on "deceptive marketing" and enrolling GIs looks good but ultimately mostly panders to public interest in fraud at for-profit colleges while still allowing the for-profit college sector to thrive. Real reform would be waged through the more complicated processes of legislative changes with regards to how much profit for-profit colleges are allowed to generate from student loan money (currently 90 percent) and through greater oversight of accreditation agencies that allow schools like those owned by Laureate to access federal student aid coffers. Hillary Clinton has chosen a middle way that may sound progressive but that, in the long term, leaves the interests of her wealthy donors untouched. (Despite marked enrollment declines in the sector in the United States, investors think international growth will remain strong.)

Meanwhile, Hillary has released a plan aimed at mitigating student loan debt. Americans now collectively owe $1 trillion in student loan debt. The big numbers have captured the public's imagination as well as those of politicians, since the issue so directly affects those middle-class voters that politicians are fond of rhetorically courting. Clinton takes aim at that sweet spot with a New College Compact that cobbles together many pre-existing proposals with some new additions: free community college, incentives for states to reverse higher education subsidy cuts, a streamlined process for repayment based on income, and incentives for states to provide tuition assistance at public colleges that do not offer loans for the neediest students. Newer ideas include a yet-to-be-detailed plan to increase subsidized day care on college campuses and make federal student aid available for short-term unaccredited "nontraditional programs," like technology coding boot camps. The compact is the kind of mixed bag that sounds good but does not show a critical feminist understanding of how and why so many people owe so much for college.

As University of Wisconsin sociologist Sara Goldrick-Rab and others have pointed out, the total cost of going to college is more than just tuition.[3] And it's the "more than tuition" part where social inequalities become most stark. Housing, transportation and living costs are increasing across the nation. More than just the cost of tuition, the high price of affording the choice to go to college by having secure housing, food, and life provisions makes student loans attractive to those who can afford them the least. Here is where for-profit colleges have innovated. Knowing that their likely student typically cannot afford the real cost of attending college, many for-profit colleges accelerate degree programs. When these schools market themselves as "fast tracks" to "a real career," they are tapping into the need that millions have to minimize the cost of choosing college. Hillary's plan does not address that growing divide. The New College Compact isn't bad so much as it is incoherent about the cause and effect of student loan debt: inequalities not just in opportunity and outcomes but inequalities writ large.

None of this makes me trust Hillary to be a real leader in higher education policy, one of the areas I know and care most about.

But these problems suggest other problems with Hillary's brand of feminism, in my view. For me, an intersectional (though admittedly a pragmatic) feminist politics would make the radical suggestion that student loan debt is a symptom of inequality but that addressing it will not solve inequality. Rather than focus on gender disparities in income, which matter but affect some women more than others, I keep a flame lit for a feminist politics that focuses on gender disparities in wealth. Income is about the present and the future. Wealth tends to be about the past. And it is the specter of the past that haunts policies aimed at equal opportunity that effectively calcify and intensify race, class, and gender inequalities.

Mainstream, professional feminism, the sort of feminism that nourishes unbridled enthusiasm at the idea of Hillary Clinton as president of the United States, has little to say about this. Mainstream, professional feminism's "can you have it all" navel-gazing fixation on the issues of high achieving, mostly white and heterosexual Western women loves to talk about income and college debt in the narrow ways that Hillary's platform demonstrates. My ambivalence about that approach can be summed up neatly: having it all is for those who already have enough. Feminist politics for those who don't—those without nearly enough access to health and wealth and safety—are sorely lacking in this most recent iteration of the Clinton twofer.

All that is part of the reason why I don't trust Hillary to give much of a damn about African American women, but it is not the only reason I don't. Being an astute politician, when Hillary ran for president in 2008, she did what she was supposed to do. She tried to win. In the South Carolina primaries Bill Clinton, one of the two in the Clinton twofer and a Hillary surrogate par excellence, went full racist dog whistle. Bill accused Barack Obama of feeding news media frenzy about race "issues" to cast him and Hillary in a bad (i.e., racist) light. It was high-level reverse racism trolling. It was classic Southern strategy rhetoric, in a state where the Southern strategy has a storied history, in a political moment when the black vote could not be easily taken for granted by a white guy who knows all the words to some Negro spirituals. It was racist in that implicit way that these things often are: that is to say, it relied on the existing racist logics and frames to do all the work. In the hands of a carpetbagger it might have been crasser. In the hands of a less-gifted politician, it might have been more transparently racist, not subtle enough. But this was Bill. Bill is from the Old South. He knows the rhythms of black speech, black rhetoric and black political narratives. Bill played his intimate relationship with Southern racial logics during his own presidential run better than he ever played that poor saxophone. Bill, better than almost any politician in recent political history, knew exactly what he was doing— signaling to white voters that Hillary was all about them—and had the skill to do it cleanly. Black voters knew it. South Carolina congressman Jim Clyburn, a longtime Clinton supporter, knew it.

Clyburn, an African American of the same Old South variety as Bill, said Bill could stand to tone down his dog whistles. As for Hillary, she was less subtle, making a comment that seemed to minimize Martin Luther King Jr.'s role in the civil rights movement: "Dr. King's dream began to be realized when President Johnson passed the Civil Rights Act. It took a president to get it done."[4]

Bernie won't take the primary where I may vote for him. Hillary has the money, the political acumen and power to go all the way. In the general election, I'm as likely to vote for her as anyone. If I do, it will be with the same resignation with which black voters, especially black women, have been voting for Democrats for years. I'll do it knowing that she will think my vote disposable. I'll do it with the image of her wagging her finger at young black activists affiliated with Black Lives Matter during a stop on her campaign. I'll do it remembering South Carolina and Laureate. I will know that she is like most politicians in this regard but that unlike most of them, she wants me to believe I owe her more consideration because we're both women, sisters in the struggle. And as black women have also been doing for millennia, I will let that stand for want of a better choice.

SEVEN

The Clintons' War on Drugs:
Why Black Lives Didn't Matter

Donna Murch

I n August 2015, an uncomfortable encounter between Black Lives Matter (BLM) protestors and Hillary Clinton finally broke the silence of many mainstream press outlets on the Clintons' shared responsibility for the disastrous policies of mass incarceration and its catalyst, the war on drugs. Although a number of prominent academics have written on the subject, little popular discussion of the racial impact of the Clintons' crime and punishment policies emerged until the opening volleys of the 2016 presidential race.[1]

A grainy cell phone video of the incident showed a handful of young BLM protestors confronting Hillary Clinton on the campaign trail in New Hampshire. After expressing her ardent feminism and pride in meeting a female presidential candidate, BLM's Daunasia Yancey forcefully confronted Clinton about her shared culpability in America's destructive war on drugs: "You and your family have been personally and politically responsible for policies that have caused health and human services disasters in impoverished communities of color through the domestic and international war on drugs that you championed as first lady, senator and secretary of state." Yancey continued, "And so I just want to know how you feel about your role in that violence, and how you plan to reverse it?"[2]

Yancey's question deftly turned Hillary's use of her husband's presidency as political qualification on its head: If her term as first lady deeply involved in policy issues qualifies her for the presidency, then she could be held responsible for policies made during those years. The Clintons had used the concept of personal responsibility to shame poor blacks for their economic predicament. Indeed, Bill Clinton titled his notorious welfare to work legislation "The Personal Responsibility and Work Opportunity Reconciliation Act of 1996." Yancey's question forced the Democratic front-runner to accept personal responsibility for mass incarceration policies passed under Bill Clinton's administration.

Hillary Clinton's response to the activists was telling. She attributed the policies of mass incarceration and the war on drugs to "the very real concerns" of communities of color and poor people, who faced a crime wave in the 1980s and 1990s. Echoing an argument that is gaining greater purchase in certain elite circles as the movement against racialized state violence and incarceration sweeps across the US, Clinton deflected the charge of anti-black animus back onto African Americans themselves.[3] It is hard to interpret her explanation as anything more than self-serving revisionism. As I demonstrate in this essay, the rush to incarcerate was fueled by much less generous motives than the ones Clinton presents. With the Clintons at the helm of the "New Democrats," their strident anti-crime policies, like their assault on welfare, reflected a cynical attempt to win back centrist white voters, especially those from Dixie and the South Central United States.[4]

A true paradox lies at the heart of the Clinton legacy. Both Hillary and Bill continue to enjoy enormous popularity among African Americans despite the devastating legacy of a presidency that resulted in the impoverishment and incarceration of hundreds of thousands of poor and working-class black people. Most shockingly, the total numbers of state and federal inmates grew more rapidly under Bill Clinton than under any other president, including the notorious Republican drug warriors Richard Nixon, Ronald Reagan, and George H. W. Bush. This fact alone should at least make one pause before granting unquestioning fealty to Hillary, but of course there are many others, including her entry into electoral politics through the 1964 Goldwater campaign, resolute support for the Violent Crime Control and Law Enforcement Act, race-baiting tactics in the 2008 election, and close ties to lobbyists for the private prison industry.[5] Nevertheless, until the encounter with BLM protestors in August 2015, few publicly called out the Clintons' shared culpability for our contemporary prison nation that subjects a third of African American men to a form of correctional control in their lifetime.[6]

The United States' historically unprecedented carceral edifice of policing and prisons has been long in the making. However, in the 1990s, the Clintons and their allies, as the quintessential "New Democrats," played a crucial role in its expansion. Like their Republican predecessors, punishing America's most vulnerable populations[7] became an important means to repudiate the democratic upheaval of the postwar years that toppled statutory Jim Crow and challenged some of the most enduring social inequities of the US. In the three decades that followed the passage of the Voting Rights Act, the drug war and its companion legislation, welfare reform, criminalized poor and working class populations of color in huge numbers, subjecting many not only to the "carceral consequences" of voter disfranchisement but also to permanent exclusion from the legal economy.[8]

While this is often understood as the quotidian cruelty of a brave neoliberal world, very specific political motives underlay policies of extreme cruelty and state-sanctioned murder in the late twentieth century.

Although they are rarely mentioned in the same breath, the escalation of America's drug war in the 1990s and the rise of the Democratic Leadership Council (DLC) and its benighted son Bill Clinton are all intimately linked. Understanding why tough-on-crime policies and welfare reform became so foundational to the vision of the New Democrats requires a look at the sensibilities that undergirded their strategy for regaining the White House and national power. As the Democratic Party reinvented itself in the aftermath of Ronald Reagan's sweeping electoral victory in 1984, Al From, an aide of Louisiana representative Gilles Long with abiding ties to big business, Governors Bruce Babbitt (Arizona) and Charles Robb (Virginia) came together with Florida senator Lawton Chiles and congressional representatives Richard Gephardt (Missouri), Sam Nunn (Georgia), and James R. Jones (Oklahoma) to launch the DLC in February 1985. The DLC's coterie of conservative and centrist politicians, who hailed overwhelmingly from citadels of white discontent in the Sunbelt and Midwest, sought to wrest the party away from its alleged liberal dominance.[9]

In terms of structural changes, they targeted the 1968 reforms to the Democratic Party's nomination process that established interest group–based organizations. By 1982 the Democratic National Committee (DNC) recognized seven different intraparty caucuses modeled on specific demographics, including "women, blacks, Hispanics, Asians, gays, liberals and business/professionals."[10] The DLC founders wanted to abandon this pluralistic party base, elevate the power of national elected officials, and pursue stronger ties with wealthy corporate donors.[11]

To diagnose the precise causes behind the Democrats' catastrophic loss of every state in the Union to Ronald Reagan in 1984, with the exception of Walter Mondale's home state of Minnesota, the DNC sponsored several research surveys, including one that has been estimated, at that time, to be the most expensive study commissioned in its history. Chair Paul Kirk paid survey researchers Milton Kotler and Nelson Rosenbaum a quarter of a million dollars to conduct a massive survey of 5,000 voters. In focus groups, whites from the South and Northern ethnic enclaves described the Democratic Party as the "give away party, giving white tax money to blacks and poor people." The explicit racist content of Kotler and Rosenbaum's report proved so embarrassing to Kirk that he suppressed its release and had nearly all of the existing copies destroyed.[12] Nevertheless, the findings made their way into DLC party policy as New Democrat fellow travelers like Thomas and Mary Edsall and Harry McPherson made similar, if more carefully veiled, arguments. McPherson, a former member of the Johnson administration, published a November 1988 op-ed essay in the *New York Times* entitled simply "How Race Destroyed the Democrats' Coalition."[13]

At the core of this anger about the shift in the Democratic Party was not just "race" as an abstraction, which too often functioned as a polite euphemism, but rather black people themselves. Another DNC-commissioned study by Stanley Greenberg, who subsequently became a pollster for Clinton in 1992, cited data from Macomb County, a suburb of Detroit, to make this point even more explicitly. "These white Democratic defectors express a profound distaste for blacks, a sentiment that pervades almost everything they think about government and politics," explained Greenberg. "Blacks constitute the explanation for their [white defectors'] vulnerability and almost everything that has gone wrong in their lives, not being black is what constitutes being middle class, not being black is what makes a neighborhood a decent place to live."[14]

Bolstered with polling data and the crisis of the Reagan landslide, the New Democrats searched for ways to aggressively distance themselves from "blacks" and to entice resentful white swing voters back into the fold. To do this, the New Democrats appropriated hot button issues from the Republican Party, later deemed "dog whistle politics," that invoked the specter of blackness without directly naming it. While the turn from welfare to work and personal responsibility is often discussed in this respect, equally important is the extensive role played by Bill Clinton and his allies in vastly expanding carceral policies, including the war on drugs, the federal death penalty, and national funding for policing and prisons in the years after the Reagan and Bush presidencies.[15]

Associated with the DLC's early stirrings, Bill Clinton did not become integrally involved until after Michael Dukakis's presidential defeat in 1988.[16] In a notorious ad campaign that drew on enduring racist imagery, George H. W. Bush won the election by blaming the Massachusetts governor for the brutal rape of a white woman by Willie Horton, a black prisoner participating in a prison furlough program. Bush advisor Lee Atwater created a vicious media blitz that featured a voice-over description of the assault paired with a menacing black-and-white mugshot of Horton. After contrasting Dukakis's opposition to the death penalty with Bush's ardent support for it, the television spot closed with the words "Weekend Prison Passes—Dukakis on Crime."[17] Atwater's race-baiting appeal proved wildly successful. As legal scholar Jonathan Simon has argued, George H. W. Bush's election "marked the emergence, for the first time, of the war on crime as the primary basis for choosing a president."[18]

Chastened by Dukakis' defeat, Bill Clinton emerged as the Southern golden boy of the New Democrats by 1990. While serving as governor of Arkansas, he became the DLC's first chair outside the Beltway. Clinton traveled nonstop and worked tirelessly to build a national infrastructure that encompassed over two dozen state-level chapters. Two years later, his rousing speech at the DLC's national conference in Cleveland, Ohio, earned him a direct line to the nomination.[19] New Democrat stalwart Sam Nunn's early endorsement played a key role, as did that of lesser known members of the DLC fold, among them African American representatives John Lewis (GA), Mike Espy (MI), William Jefferson (LA), and Floyd Flake (NY). In a depressingly familiar pattern from the Reagan administration, the support of an elite sector of the black political class helped to legitimize hard-line anti-crime policy that proved devastating for low-income populations of color.[20]

Prior to his entrée onto the national stage, Clinton's governorship of Arkansas demonstrated how embracing the death penalty paved the Democrats' road back to power. After a comparatively liberal first term in which he granted over seventy separate sentencing commutations, Clinton radically reversed his earlier stance after his Republican opponent won largely by smearing him in the eyes of the electorate as considerate of criminals. Upon returning to the governor's mansion in 1982, Clinton parsed out a meager seven additional commutations over a ten-year span, and none for the death penalty. Indeed, in 1992 amid massive press coverage, Bill flew back to Arkansas days before the New Hampshire primary to preside over the execution of Rickey Ray Rector, a black man convicted of killing a white police officer. Rector had shot himself through the temple, forcing surgeons to remove over three inches of the frontal lobe of his brain. He was so cognitively impacted as a result of the surgery that he set aside the dessert from his last meal to eat after his lethal injection. Rickey even told a reporter that he planned to vote for Bill Clinton in the fall.[21]

As the governor of a Southern state, Clinton's execution of Rector was a powerful symbolic act that refuted incumbent president George Bush Sr.'s attempt to cast Bill Clinton and his running mate, Al Gore, as soft on crime. In the words of political kingmaker David Garth, Clinton "had someone put to death who had only part of a brain. You can't find them any tougher than that."[22] Far from gratuitous cruelty, Rector's execution and the virulent and racially discriminatory policies that followed it were the ultimate indication that the post–civil rights Democratic Party had repudiated its marginal commitment not only to black equality, but to black life itself. Between 1994 and 1999, nearly two thirds of the people sentenced to the federal death penalty were black—a rate nearly seven times that of their representation in the American population.[23]

Today, the death penalty haunts the edges of American politics, but at the height of the country's rush to mass incarcerate, executions became central to the rightward drift of the Democratic Party. Once in office, Bill Clinton made sixty new crimes eligible for the death penalty and fellow Democrats bragged about their specific additions to the list.[24] Joe Biden mused that "someone asleep for the last twenty years might wake up to think that Republicans were represented by Abbie Hoffman" and the Democrats by J. Edgar Hoover.[25]

As president, Bill Clinton and his allies embarked on a draconian punishment campaign to outflank the Republicans. "I can be nicked a lot, but no one can say that I'm soft on crime," he bragged.[26] Roughly a year and a half after the 1992 Los Angeles Rebellion—the largest civil disturbance in US history, in which demonstrators took to the streets for six straight days to protest the acquittal of the officers involved in the Rodney King beating—Clinton passed the Violent Crime Control and Law Enforcement Act. At its core, this legislation was a federal "three strikes" bill that established a $30.2 billion Crime Trust Fund to allocate monies for state and municipal police and prison expansion. Like its predecessors, starting with Johnson's Omnibus Crime Control and Safe Streets Act, the federal government provided funding to accelerate punitive policies at all levels of governance. Specific provisions included monies for placing 100,000 new police on the streets, the expansion of death penalty eligible crimes, lifetime imprisonment for people who committed a third violent federal felony offense with two prior state or federal felony convictions, gang "enhancements" in sentencing for federal defendants, allowing children as young as thirteen to be prosecuted as adults in special cases, and the Violence Against Women Act.[27]

Hillary strongly supported this legislation and stood resolutely behind her husband's punishment campaign. "We need more police, we need more and tougher prison sentences for repeat offenders," Hillary declared in 1994. "The 'three strikes and you're out' for violent offenders has to be part of the plan. We need more prisons to keep violent offenders for as long as it takes to keep them off the streets," she added.[28] Elsewhere, she remarked, "We will finally be able to say, loudly and clearly, that for repeat, violent, criminal offenders: three strikes and you're out."[29]

Like his notorious Republican predecessors, Clinton imposed a toxic mix of punishment and withdrawal of social welfare, but with a difference. The Democratic president actually implemented these policies on a much larger scale than the Republican New Right. According to *New Jim Crow* author Michelle Alexander, "Far from resisting the emergence of the new caste system" that Ronald Reagan had codified into law through the Anti-Drug Abuse Acts of 1986 and 1988, "Clinton escalated the drug war beyond what conservatives had imagined possible a decade earlier."[30]

In the 1980s and 1990s, incarceration became de facto urban policy for impoverished communities of color in America's cities. Legislation was passed to impose mandatory minimums, deny public housing to entire families if any member was even suspected of a drug crime, expand federal death-penalty-eligible crimes, and impose draconian restrictions of parole. Ultimately, multiple generations of America's most vulnerable populations, including drug users, African Americans, Latinos, and the very poor found themselves confined to long-term prison sentences and lifelong social and economic marginality.[31] The carceral effects of the New Democrats' competition with the Republicans vastly increased the ranks of the incarcerated. State and federal prisons imprisoned more people under the Clintons' watch than under any previous administration. During his two terms the inmate population grew from roughly 1.3 million to 2 million, and the number of executions to 98 by 1999.[32] Significantly, the Democratic president even refused to support the Congressional Black Caucus's proposed Racial Justice Act, which would have prevented discriminatory application of the death penalty.[33]

Despite this terrible record of racialized punishment for political gain, the Clintons' peculiar ability to reinvent themselves has erased memory of many of their past misdeeds. This is nowhere more true than within the African American community, in which a combination of Bill Clinton's high-profile black political appointments, his obvious comfort in the presence of black people, and the cultural symbolism of his saxophone performance on Arsenio Hall's talk show has severely distorted the New Democrats' true legacy for the black majority. After all, Toni Morrison, African American Nobel Laureate for literature, embraced Bill Clinton as America's "first black president," even if only in jest.

At a deeper structural level, the constraints of the two-party system have resulted in black Americans' political capture inside the Democratic Party, in which no viable electoral alternative exists. Frederick Douglass said of the party of Lincoln during Reconstruction, "The Republican Party is the ship, all else is the sea." And so it is, with Democrats in the era of mass incarceration. Equally important is the sharp class polarization inside the African American community in which a select group of black elites understand their fate as wholly bound up with the leadership of the Democratic Party. The Clinton presidency is a cautionary tale in this respect. The couple's close relationships with Vernon Jordan and other black insiders offered an illusion of access that superseded any real concern for how hard-line anti-crime, drug war, and welfare policies affected poor and working class African Americans. As the movement against state-sanctioned violence and for black lives grows, it is important to remember that proximity to power rarely equals real power.

In American politics we so often live in an eternal present. Forgotten are the days of the DLC, which was dismantled in 2011 at the close of President Barack Obama's first term. In many respects, the DLC had become archaic, precisely because contemporary Democrats have so fully incorporated, and even expanded, the bitter fruit of the Reagan revolution. Former Federal Reserve chairman and Ayn Rand enthusiast Alan Greenspan once described Bill Clinton as "the best Republican president we've had in a while."[34] More recently, Barack Obama praised Ronald Reagan for correcting "the excesses of the 1960s and 1970s."[35]

As both parties have engaged in a steady march to the right over the past three decades, it is not surprising that the Clintons have done little more than offer halfhearted mea culpas about their role in the drug war and mass incarceration. In July 2015, Bill Clinton went before the National Association for the Advancement of Color People's 106th annual convention to admit that his federal drug and anti-crime policy made the problem of mass incarceration worse, especially at the state level. Many journalists interpreted his candor cynically as advance preparation for his wife's presidential campaign of 2016.[36] As in so many things the Clintons have done, even their disavowals appear to be self-serving. Hillary's explanation that a crime wave inside low-income communities of color motivated her husband's escalation of domestic wars on drugs and crime hides the Clintons' shared role in capitulating to racist rhetoric and policy in the 1990s. Indeed, they used the drug war, and mass incarceration more broadly, as a powerful political tool to rebuild conservative white support for the Democratic Party. It is only because the experiences of the incarcerated and the poor have been so profoundly erased that the Clintons can be thought of as liberals (racial or otherwise) in any respect.[37]

As we approach the 2016 election, it would be good to remember the human consequences of the Clintons' "tough on crime" stance, and how Hillary has tried to replicate this strategy of "strength and experience" again and again to prove her appropriateness as both a female presidential contender and a blue dog Democrat. Candidate Clinton has embraced hardness as political qualification, as evidenced by her proclamation "We came, we saw, he died," about the killing of Muammar Gaddafi; her threat to obliterate Iran; or her embellished Bosnian sniper story.[38] As mainstream feminist icon, Hillary has more in common with Britain's Iron Lady Margaret Thatcher or the European Union's austerity champion Angela Merkel than her beloved Eleanor Roosevelt. If the history of the war on drugs is any indicator, however, outstripping Republican belligerence from the right will not end well for the rest of us.

EIGHT

Marry the State, Jail the People: Hillary Clinton and the Rise of Carceral Feminism

Yasmin Nair

That anything to do with what is known as the "prison industrial complex" and its spread would occupy the attention of politicians would have seemed unthinkable in the run-up to the US presidential election of 2012. But by 2015, the topic had become so widely discussed that even Republican candidates such as Carly Fiorina and Rand Paul had come out against lengthy sentences for minor infractions like marijuana possession. In fact, one televised Republican debate in 2015 sounded like a *New Jim Crow* book group, with several uttering the phrase "mass incarceration" as if it were a bad thing.

Sure, much of it is political posturing and none of these candidates want to abolish the prison system. It's unlikely that either Republicans or Democrats—even a libertarian like Paul or a democratic socialist like Bernie Sanders—have given up their punitive ways.[1] Still, where previous election years have seen candidates focusing on how their rivals were insufficiently harsh on criminals—the first Bush

infamously used the story of Willie Horton to win the presidency—
this time around, there is an eagerness to demonstrate awareness that
the US's current rate of incarceration is a source of shame, not pride.
Hillary Clinton sang along eagerly with this chorus of denuncia-
tion, calling for an end to "an era of incarceration" in April 2015. But
this was awkward. For one thing, some of her campaign bundlers
also work, directly or indirectly, for the private prison industry.[2] But
more deeply at odds with Clinton's new Angela Davis imperson-
ation was this embarrassing set of facts: her record.

Let's acknowledge that Clinton faces a dilemma as a prominent
woman making her second bid for the presidency: she must temper
her need to prove that she can be an aggressive, militaristic commander in chief with evidence that her womanly sensitivities remain
unscathed. Positioning herself as a carceral feminist—one willing to
get tough on criminals in order to protect girls and women—has
long been central to Clinton's navigation of gendered shoals such
as these.

Clinton's feminism occupies a central place in the public's perception of her and in terms of how she negotiates the landscape of
"women's issues." That landscape is vastly different even from her
first campaign in 2008. Domestically, the question of campus rape
and related matters of sexual assault occupy the public imagination.
Emma Sulkowicz, a Columbia University art student, captured
attention with her Carry That Weight project, in which she vowed
to—and until she graduated, did—carry her mattress around as
long as her accused rapist remained on campus. She was even invited
to Barack Obama's 2014 State of the Union address. Slutwalk, a
transnational protest of rape, rejecting the prevalent moralizing over
victims' manner of dress, began in 2011 and remains a prominent,
if contested, annual event. Accusations against unnamed University
of Virginia fraternity brothers capture headlines; even prominent
entertainment figures such as Bill Cosby, Roman Polanski, and
Woody Allen are not immune.

In all of this, the prison industrial complex looms large in both obvious and unseen, sometimes insidious ways. The most prominent campaigns against violence, like the one around campus sexual assaults, tend to focus on imprisonment and sentencing as the best solutions. As Kristin Bumiller notes in her richly contextual book *In an Abusive State: How Neoliberalism Appropriated the Feminist Movement Against Sexual Violence,* the drive towards such carceral punishment began as an attempt to find resources for women in a patriarchal system of jurisprudence which gave them no recourse even in cases of rape. Over the past few decades, social service agencies which concentrate on the most marginalized, including women in domestic violence situations and trafficked and undocumented immigrant labor, have become legally compelled to call upon the carceral state as first recourse.

The overall effect is a landscape of feminist carcerality which draws upon the force of the state acting in collusion with social service agencies, emboldened by an angry clamoring for "justice" in mostly privileged sites like college campuses. The end result is that some women, mostly middle to upper class, and mostly white, are able to demand punitive measures for their accused attackers, but vast numbers of other women, mostly poor, often women of color, are left to struggle under a combination of poverty and vulnerability created by the very system that claims to protect them.[3] At the same time that some women are granted the right to invoke state involvement and send more people to prison, millions of others—mostly poor white and black women—increasingly feel the brunt of a carceral regime. According to the Sentencing Project, from 1980 to 2010 the number of women in prison has increased at nearly 1.5 times the rate for men, a 646 percent rise which means that now nearly 205,000 women are incarcerated. Nearly 75 percent of women in prison have mental health problems, in contrast to 55 percent of men—and the significantly large numbers across the board say a lot about how the prison industrial complex is also now the dumping ground for a broken health care system. In all but thirteen states, incarcerated women delivering babies are shackled during the process of birth.[4]

Pregnancy and abortion are increasingly criminalized and can lead to incarceration. Purvi Patel of Indiana was sentenced to twenty years for feticide after a self-induced abortion/miscarriage, despite no plausible evidence that the fetus had been alive at the time of birth. Emily Bazelon has pointed out that Patel is only one of many women being prosecuted for such supposed crimes.[5]

In Oklahoma, Tondalo Hall received a thirty-year sentence for failing to protect her children from the abusive boyfriend who broke her three-month-old daughter's ribs and femur.[6] In other words, the very carceral state that was in some part meant to protect women and their dependents is now being used to police, surveil, and incarcerate them, along with countless men and transgender people. This seemingly contradictory situation has brought about what scholars including Elizabeth Bernstein and Janet Halley refer to as "carceral feminism" or "governmental feminism": the idea that feminism functions most efficiently when it can be aided and abetted by enforcing the mechanism of the law and its most punitive methods. Broadly, these terms describe how the interests and safety of women are protected through a rigorous and, some would argue, lethal system, to supposedly end gender-based crimes.[7]

Clinton, as a female candidate and someone who has sought to establish her credentials as a feminist politician, has played a significant role in the expansion of carceral feminism. She coined the notorious phrase "Eight years of Bill, eight years of Hill," and she made no secret of her active role in her husband's presidency.[8] As the couple attempted to win reelection, they escalated their use of the law to define and protect or to exclude and intimidate populations through such measures as the 1993 North American Free Trade Agreement, the 1994 Violence against Women Act, the 1996 Antiterrorism and Effective Death Penalty Act, and the 1996 Illegal

Immigration Reform and Immigrant Responsibility Act. Their harmful effects can still be felt decades later.

For the most part, discussions of Clinton's record on the international stage have been divorced from discussions of her work on the domestic front. This essay, based on the assumption that Clinton bears some responsibility for what was enacted during her husband's two terms, will examine the ways in which both these tracks of her career in fact have melded and influenced one another. Taken together, what emerges is a picture of how Clinton's military stance abroad and her policies at home intertwine to produce a particularly virulent strain of carceral feminism.

The statistics have been repeated so often now that they form a natural backdrop to any discussion of the prison industrial complex: the US is home to only 5 percent of the world's population but holds 25 percent of the world's prison population. There are 2.4 million behind bars, but, overall, more than 7 million people are tethered to the penal system in some way (parole, house arrest, etc.).

The logic of the prison permeates our national consciousness and cultural representations. In the last few years, the prison industrial complex has become a popular and even, dare I say, sexy topic. *Orange Is the New Black,* a Netflix show about a women's minimum-security prison that premiered in 2013, stars the transgender actor Laverne Cox who is also now an occasional spokesperson on trans prison issues. One of the most common ways to describe the phenomenon of mass incarceration is to call it "the New Jim Crow," after the widely cited book by Michelle Alexander. Prisons occupy an uneasy place in the American imagination. They are sites, increasingly, of violence and mayhem, and at once places where people supposedly go to learn better and from which no one escapes. There is, of course, no sense in which prison can ever be a good place for any reason; it dehumanizes and demoralizes people and does little to help them on their way (if they ever get out). This is not to say that we cannot and must not fight for what might make lives more bearable for those trapped inside, but this essay is based on the assumption that there is no reforming the penal system. Everywhere, it seems, the prison industrial complex is under attack. Undocumented immigrants have been staging protests outside detention centers, and transgender rights activists have disrupted Obama's speeches, insisting that trans prisoners should be let out. In 2014 and 2015, the brutal murders of mostly black young men and women in public or their suspicious deaths while behind bars have become unavoidable topics of public discussion. Such deaths have occurred for decades, but what's different now is that they can now be quickly recorded and disseminated like never before, forcing a sometimes-reluctant public to take note.

Hillary Clinton's policies, including those she executed alongside her husband, have contributed to this carceral landscape. In 1994, the Clintons oversaw the passage of the North American Free Trade Agreement (NAFTA). As a result of US goods flooding local markets, Mexican merchants and farmers, whether selling textiles or corn, have been forced to shut down. Approximately 2 million farmers had to abandon their occupations, and today 25 million Mexicans live in "food poverty." As Laura Carlsen of the Center for International Policy points out, "Transnational industrial corridors in rural areas have contaminated rivers and sickened the population and typically, women bear the heaviest impact." Restrictive trade policies, disguised as "free trade," mean the displacement of millions of people who had up to that point been able to survive and thrive in their native economies. NAFTA eventually caused massive waves of immigration as desperate Mexicans streamed across the border.[9]

The Clintons' method of working with what was now a migrant/ refugee crisis was to initiate the draconian Illegal Immigration Reform and Immigrant Responsibility Act and the Antiterrorism and Effective Death Penalty Act, both in 1996. Scholars Rebecca Bohrman and Naomi Murakawa point out that while the latter was supposed to tackle domestic terrorism in response to the Oklahoma

City bombing, it has in fact "justified immigration restrictions in criminological terms and criminal penalties in anti-immigration terms."[10] Taken together, the legislation increased the penalties for what were formerly relatively minor infractions and expanded the reach of the prison industrial complex. For instance, before 1996, undocumented immigrants apprehended and imprisoned for crimes were released after serving their sentences. After 1996, they would remain in prison until deported. Minor offenses, such as driving under the influence or filing a false tax return, would now be classified as "aggravated felonies" and place immigrants on the fast track to deportation.

As 1996 was the year that the Clintons had to work on getting Bill reelected, they began preparing by ratcheting up a socially and economically conservative set of policies under the guise of supposedly more enlightened "New Democrat" principles. They set in place the Personal Responsibility and Work Opportunity Reconciliation Act of 1996, otherwise known as the Welfare Reform Act, which created Temporary Assistance to Needy Families. This allowed states to determine their own welfare programs, with the worst effects on the poorest, mostly women, single mothers, and mostly African Americans. As Bohrman and Murakawa point out, it also singled out immigrants and drug convicts: "Cutting benefits to immigrants, both undocumented and legal, was at the heart of welfare reform." The Illegal Immigration Reform and Immigrant Responsibility Act made undocumented immigrants ineligible for food stamps, and the Personal Responsibility Act also excluded legal immigrants from benefits such as food stamps. In addition, the Illegal Immigration Reform and Immigrant Responsibility Act instituted the three- and ten-year bars. This meant that immigrants who lived in the US illegally for a period of six months to a year would be deported and barred from reentry for three years; those who had lived illegally in the US for more than a year would be deported and prevented from reentry for ten years.

These laws worked along with the omnibus Violent Crime Control and Law Enforcement Act of 1994, which instituted "reforms" such as the Three Strikes provision; they had the cumulative effect of increasing the vulnerability of the most impoverished and in-need populations, including citizens, legal immigrants, and the undocumented. In October 2015, Virginia Sole-Smith reported on the aftereffects of welfare reform for *Harper's Magazine*:

> Welfare reform has been successful by one measure alone: it has reduced government spending. In 1995, about 14 million Americans were on welfare; today, that number is down to 4.2 million. Meanwhile, the benefits received by families with no other cash income now bring them to less than half the federal poverty line, according to research by the Center on Budget and Policy Priorities. In 2014, the median family of three on welfare received a monthly check of just $428, and other government assistance programs have seen their budgets slashed even further. For every hundred families with children that are living in poverty, sixty-eight were able to access cash assistance before Bill Clinton's welfare reform. By 2013, that number had fallen to twenty-six.

The Clintons' successor in the White House, George W. Bush, tweaked welfare reform during his term in office, adding provisions that made it even harder for women in particular to keep their benefits and support their families and dependents. These included prioritizing marriage as a public policy goal by, for instance, encouraging single mothers to stay in relationships with their children's fathers and redirecting welfare money into marriage classes for poor people.[11] Critics of such measures often blame them on the Bush years, conveniently forgetting that Bush was merely using a Clinton-led legislative agenda as a template.

It is safe to say that the combined and cumulative effect of all the legislation set in place by the Clintons in their efforts to appear tough on crime, the poor, immigrants, and potential "terrorists" was to create a massive and deeply impoverished population. The effect of the return bars has been the creation of a massive pool of people barely eking out a living as undocumented immigrants in the US but too desperate to leave because of their fear of not being allowed to reunite with the friends and family they have here. In other words, undocumented immigrants from Mexico and Asia have much less mobility than the goods and services that are so freely "traded" under legislation such as NAFTA.

In 1994 the Clintons were instrumental in passing the Violence Against Women Act, which has been criticized by prison abolitionists, criminal justice reformers and left feminists for its reliance on mandatory arrest laws that have expanded jail and prison populations. The Violence Against Women Act continues to be a bone of contention: mainstream feminists praise it for making it possible for women, especially undocumented immigrants, to report their abusers and/or sex traffickers. But feminists on the left, such as Beth Richie, point out that the legislation makes criminal prosecution and incarceration the first step in cases like those of alleged domestic abuse or trafficking. It is premised on an uncomplicated analysis of power and social structures and does not allow for the fact that not all those defined as victims want to use prison as a first option. The legislation has also expanded the role of the prison industrial complex into the lives of many women for whom, as Richie has pointed out, "the legal system is not a supportive, or even a fair, system," black women or immigrants, for example.[12]

The effects of all this legislation still linger, but Clinton has continued to shine in her role as the figurehead of carceral feminism and has brought it overseas in the name of "human rights."

In 2011, she gave a speech to the United Nations, as secretary of state, affirming that "gay rights are human rights." In it, Clinton deftly combined a sweeping idea of gay rights with veiled threats of countries being punished for not adhering to the US notion of what constitutes a gay rights agenda. Clinton's words were in part a direct response to a bill being debated in Uganda that would criminalize homosexuality and make it eligible for a death sentence. In effect, Clinton was threatening to cut off aid to countries that did not hew to US-defined ideas of "gay rights." In this, she (along with David Cameron, who made similar pronouncements at the time) chose to ignore a statement made by fifty African organizations two months prior: in October 2011, African activists implored the West not to enact economic measures that would harm the most vulnerable in their countries, including lesbians, gay, bisexual, and transgender (LGBT) people, and pointed out that laws criminalizing homosexuality were based on colonial legacies of homophobia.[13] But Clinton has a broad base of support among mainstream gays and lesbians, and her words affirming LGBT rights everywhere are already being echoed by the Human Rights Campaign which, following the end of the gay marriage fight, has established international gay rights as its next agenda item.

Today, human rights—and women's rights along with them—have been taken up by those military complexes that have most abused them[14] and can now assert them as justification for military intervention. We might recall Laura Bush's singular radio address in 2001, justifying the bombing of Afghanistan as a way to save Afghani women from the Taliban. It is entirely likely that the next Clinton presidency will involve such acts on behalf of gays and women in other countries, but perhaps this time with finely calibrated drones designed to seek out precisely those bodies that would persecute queer bodies and women while leaving queers and women themselves magically untouched.

Such measures have far-reaching effects on the spread of a rapacious capitalism, a system that Hillary Clinton passionately defended in the first Democratic debate. In the end, capitalism itself is carceral; it is embedded in the logic of the prison just as much as the prison industrial complex is embedded in the logic of capitalism itself. An emphasis on saving the downtrodden—whether those are women on US campuses, nameless gays and lesbians and trans people elsewhere, or women ostensibly trafficked by mysterious oligarchs into brothels in dungeons—is only cover for the same laws that allow for the easy flight of capital across borders. Capital flows unimpeded while the surplus bodies, the most marginal and disposable that enable its movement, are scrutinized, surveilled, and ultimately brutalized into the ever-expanding prison industrial complex.

NINE

Abortion and the Politics of Failure

Maureen Tkacik

In 2013 or 2014, a barista at the restaurant I worked at got knocked up by the handsome crack addict sous chef she'd met while interning (that is, serving breakfast) at a homeless shelter. Although crack addict chef wanted to have the baby, he was not so delusional that he could not understand why she didn't, so he convinced his sister in Mexico City to overnight them some abortion pills. That way they could spare themselves the depressing $500 experience of procuring them at Planned Parenthood.

Should she take them? Maria looked to me, I think, as someone who had fucked up enough in life to know the difference between truly bad and merely unconventional decisions.

"Absolutely," I probably said, since "absolutely" is the stock restaurant industry response to basically every question to which "Yes, Chef" does not apply. "The only real difference between an American and Mexican pill abortion is that Planned Parenthood might, *if you're lucky*, give you a few utterly worthless Tylenol 3 pills.

So *absolutely* make sure you have *a lot* of weed and at least three or four Percocets or Vicodins before you take them."

Maria's story is a revealing parable of what the American feminist movement has accomplished in the forty-eight years since a third-year law student drove over the border to obtain the illegal procedure that would inspire her to sue Dallas attorney general Henry Wade on behalf of a client famously dubbed "Jane Roe": Not much. Although the American feminist establishment has invested hugely in money, time, and intellectual energy to ensure that women maintain the legal choice to not reproduce—while investing in very little else—that choice is still much easier to exercise in Mexico, a country where no such right exists. This is telling because Hillary Clinton owes her chances at the presidency to abortion: and she's not alone—it's often Democrats' unique selling proposition to women.

This would be somewhat less noteworthy if the American abortion rights lobby were more like labor unions or retirees or basically every other constituency historically understood to constitute the Democratic "base"—that is, chronically betrayed and abandoned by its own corrupt and amoral ruling clique—but it isn't. The abortion lobby is arguably the only Democratic Party interest group the Clintons never fucked over, and the Democratic Party's support for abortion rights in the face of the so-called Republican "War on Women" has become increasingly central to the party's messaging. During the 2014 midterm elections I had a front-row seat at that circus: a gig that involved analyzing 196 commercials aired by the Democratic Congressional Campaign Committee and its affiliated House Majority Political Action Committee, of which thirty-five consisted of depicting X Republican Candidate as a Warrior against Women—which everyone knows means abortion, since on other issues that disproportionately affect women, like health care, welfare, and wages, there is little policy consensus among Democrats. As a brand, abortion is pretty much all they've got.

And yet the clinics keep closing, the regulations become ever more onerous, and the generation most threatened by GOP misojihadists—women in their twenties account for more than half of the abortions administered in any given year—consistently exhibits indifference toward Hillary Clinton, preferring Obama by overwhelming margins in 2008 and Bernie Sanders by narrower (but still all things considered remarkable) ones in 2016 in a phenomenon Democratic National Committee chairwoman and lifetime Hillary suckup Debbie Wasserman Schultz dubbed "a complacency among the generation of young women whose entire lives have been lived after *Roe v. Wade* was decided" in an interview with Ana Marie Cox in the *New York Times Magazine*.

But what have Wasserman-Schultz and her generation actually done for abortion rights? She was all of eight years old in 1973; the number of abortion clinics in America has fallen by close to a third since she was in her twenties.[1] The official abortion rate falls to a new post-*Roe* low every year, but a 2015 survey of 779 women in Texas revealed that nearly 6 percent of respondents had either self-induced their own abortions or reported that their best friends had, most commonly with pills purchased over the counter from pharmacies in Mexico. It's fair to say the makers and distributors of Mexican misoprostol pills have done infinitely more than Hillary Clinton's political clique to ensure reality-based abortion rights during Maria's lifetime.

Reality is not perception, though, and Maria's friends at the extortionately priced university she attended on scholarship had voiced misgivings about the Mexican pills. The movement that had invested so heavily in abortion's legal codification had generated a multitude of alarmist Internet stories on the epidemic of "desperate"—and highly confused—women "forced" by the rash of new abortion laws to self-inflict illegal abortions,[2] with consequences ranging from unspeakable pain and massive blood loss to attempted murder charges.

You couldn't write that kind of tale of collective guilt about Maria, an honors student in perhaps the only municipality in America where the number of abortion providers has actually *increased* since the 2010–2014 Tea Party state house takeovers, who was merely trying to save herself some money. Thanks to her level of education, some research on the Internet, and friends like me who had gotten abortion pills the legal way, she never felt compelled to consume fifty pills or "stick them in every orifice of her body" like the nameless desperate women in the worst of the horror stories. Critically, she understood that misoprostol is *the* "active" ingredient in a Planned Parenthood pill abortion—a useful fact curiously left out of the Texas Policy Evaluation Project's somewhat melodramatic brief on the topic and most other coverage of Mexican misoprostol.[3] As for the unspeakable pain and veritable rivers of bloody discharge suffered by the do-it-yourself abortionists interviewed in those stories—we'd gone through all of that too, the legal way, and were fairly certain we didn't need to have parted with two or three weeks' rent for the experience. And in that sense, Maria's back-alley abortion seemed less like a desperate measure than a small show of empowerment. She had terminated her pregnancy with no so-called "assistance" from EMILY's List or Planned Parenthood or any other exponent of the abortion lobby.

This is important because the last and only time I ever considered voting for Hillary Clinton was also the last and only time I had an abortion. It was February 2008; I had spent the preceding year establishing Jezebel as the leading Internet destination for pro-Obama celebrity gossip and occasionally having sex with an ex-boyfriend who lived a few blocks away and disliked pulling out. Then one morning I'd puked. The clinic sends you home with four tablets; I was told to let them dissolve under my gums; about an hour later the contractions were hallucinogenic, radioactive, psychotic, profound—all the pain I would years later feel in thirty-six hours of labor condensed into about one and a half, with none of the anticipation or adrenaline or epidurally administered fentanyl. Distressed, my ex-boyfriend called the doctor to see if there was anything at all he could do about the pain. The doctor said no. And then I thought, while pondering in the moment how relatively easy Christ had had it on the cross and what a miracle it was that something so painful hadn't killed me, about the fact that there were men who would call me a *murderer* over this.

It was a revelation. I had always hated the Clintons. But for a day or two after that abortion, I finally felt like I *got* why Hillary rendered so many discerning women I otherwise respected irrational: all those *men*. Men, spouting inane theories on right-wing talk shows; filibustering on statehouse floors; slut-shaming; bombing Planned Parenthoods; hitting on interns; indiscriminately referring to various forms of contraception as "abortifacients" on Fox News; complaining about pulling out, while pulling in 140 cents on every dollar we do because of the outmoded assumption they should feel comfortable supporting the imaginary children of the abortions we didn't get, the lesser costs of which they'd never in reality deign to cough up more than 50 percent; and generally waging War on Women through a whole suite of miscellaneous microaggressions. I'll stop there. The point is, especially back when G. W. Bush was still president, I often wondered in vulnerable moments if they wouldn't have tried to genocide the whole gender, were it not for our role in perpetuating the species. And it is moments like that, experienced by so many of us, moments in which you are liable to trust a woman over virtually any man except maybe your father, that rake the campaign funds into EMILY's List.

The thing is, raising money is pretty much all the abortion lobby has achieved in the century so far. EMILY's List has raised hundreds of millions of dollars since its 1985 founding but its record is truly, improbably abysmal. In the 2006 midterm elections alone the group spent $46 million endorsing thirty House candidates, eight of whom won. They employ no actual lobbyists to sway the candidates they don't bankroll, nor do they exhibit much interest in state races that actually influence abortion policy in places like Tennessee and Texas. They have succeeded in hardening Hillary's stance on abortion rights, and if she wins it will arguably be their first victory since the FDA approved RU-486. Just how Pyrrhic a victory can American abortion rights advocates expect if she wins? A brief look back at the campaign to legalize the so-called "French" abortion pill during her husband's presidency provides a few clues.

Anyone who remembers the '90s will recall the protracted saga over the "controversial French abortion pill RU-486," as the media called it, lending it a frisson of forbidden glamor. RU-486 was supposed to revolutionize the reproductive choice landscape by giving doctors the right to administer abortions from the comfort of their own prescription pads and women the right to endure them from the privacy of their own couches, robbing the abortion wars not only of their most viciously disputed real estate—the clinic, a site to be bombed, protested, blockaded—but of the radical anti-abortion propagandists' most gruesome visual symbols. As National Right to Life Committee president Dr. John Wilke himself admitted in some of the earliest press on the pill: "We're really very simplistic, visually oriented people; if what [abortions] destroy in there doesn't look human, then it will make our job more difficult."

But none of that ever happened, because the pill did not change the abortion landscape in any significant way whatsoever. Because, inter alia, when the dysfunctional investor syndicate that controlled the rights to distribute RU-486 (mifepristone) in the United States finally won FDA approval to market the drug in September 2000, it set the price at more than $100 per pill, so that the FDA-approved regimen of three 200-milligram pills would cost more than $600, considerably more than the going rate for a first trimester surgical abortion.

The abortion industry quickly scrapped the FDA regimen for a more affordable cocktail of one 200-milligram RU-486 pill plus four 200-milligram pills of misoprostol, the so-called Mexican pill, part of a class of drugs called "prostaglandins" which stimulate uterine contractions. It was a lose–lose proposition in many respects: the cost of stocking the mifepristone alone was still way too prohibitive to attract any clinics not already in the abortion business, but by substituting more of the cheaper misoprostol, the regimen became considerably more painful. (Early clinical trials of prostaglandins as abortifacients were restricted to women who had already had children and were by extension prepared for the peculiar hell of labor pain.)

Fifteen years later fewer than 1 percent of American abortions are performed at physicians' offices, and pill abortions account for a measly 20 percent or so of abortions performed in the United States, as compared with 80–90 percent in many Western European countries.

The craziest part of all this is that RU-486 on its own does not, strictly speaking, bring about a complete abortion. Rather, it ends a pregnancy by blocking the hormone progesterone, the deficiency of which is believed to cause miscarriages in some women, but even taken four days in a row it never proved much more successful at actually expelling the embryo/fetus from the womb than a naturally occurring miscarriage would. So the drug's makers began combining it in trials with prostaglandins, which ripen the cervix and are widely used to induce labor in women who are more than forty-one-weeks pregnant and haven't gone into labor naturally, or who have suffered incomplete miscarriages. By supplementing the RU-486 regimen with the prostaglandin misoprostol, the medical cocktail quickly achieved efficacy rates of 95 percent and higher.

This was helpful, because misoprostol was cheap and widely available under the brand name Cytotec, whose maker Searle had won FDA approval in 1988 to market it as an anti-ulcer medication.

Soon enough clinicians were reporting that 200 milligrams of RU-486 was just as effective as 600 so long as one doubled the dose of Cytotec.

The French pill was taking all the credit, Maria and I joked, while the Mexican pills anonymously did all the labor—we knew all about this because we worked at a French restaurant. (And sure enough, Cytotec on its own in some clinical trials has been effective at inducing miscarriage.) But the real distinction between the two abortion pills is more like the difference between Republicans and Democrats. Cytotec, a comprehensively "American" product when it was introduced to the market, was the creation of a Republican-affiliated company and a Republican-appointed FDA: Donald Rumsfeld was Searle's CEO during eight of the fifteen years between its 1973 patent of misoprostol and its 1988 FDA approval as an ulcer medication. Over the same period, many of the company's direct competitors shut down their own prostaglandin research and manufacture under pressure from anti-abortionists, and Searle, the company once famed for peddling the first birth control pill, steadily steered its focus away from reproductive matters—pulling its two intrauterine devices from the market in 1986—and toward a more benign (and lucrative) public identity as the chemical giant behind the ubiquitous NutraSweet®. When Cytotec was up for FDA approval, the company even proposed labeling the drug dangerous for all women "of childbearing age"—language the FDA deemed overly restrictive. Still, neither Searle nor Monsanto were subjected to any serious protests or organized boycotts by anti-abortion protestors for their innocuous ulcer pill, even as one Brazilian pharmacology professor calculated in 1993 that the drug, used by itself, had induced more than 12 million abortions in its first three and a half years on the market in that country.[4] (Twenty years later the *Atlantic* wrote that somehow Brazilians had mysteriously "uncovered" the drug's secondary function as a "magic personal solution to a dreaded problem" very much "by accident," as though Searle and its competitors had not been researching prostaglandins since the 1930s specifically for their role in reproduction.[5] It's worth underscoring here that Cytotec was also a uniquely painful way to terminate a pregnancy, befitting a political philosophy that essentially holds that women who have abortions ought to be punished.) By contrast Hoechst, a German conglomerate whose French subsidiary developed (the decidedly non-painful) RU-486, was thoroughly transparent about the drug's reproductive motives and thus thoroughly crippled by the ensuing culture wars. RU-486 was the subject of numerous *New York Times* stories during the 1980s. Letters equating its new product with the industrial slaughter perpetrated by the Nazi death camp chemical giant IG Farben began barraging company headquarters, and pro-life pharmacist groups in America singled out Hoechst's most lucrative drugs for downright surgical boycotts. Caving to pressure, in 1989 Hoechst unilaterally announced it would not be distributing RU-486 outside of France. The abortion lobby then leapt into action, visiting France and gathering support from the scientific community, the American people, and the Democrats. On the 1992 campaign trail, Bill Clinton promised to bring the drug to America. And as extensive conservative think tank Freedom of Information Act requests would document, the president's new health and human services secretary Donna Shalala went right to work making good on the promise.

Donna Shalala is an individual who vividly embodies the historical and cultural inextricability of Hillaryland, the abortion lobby and Beltway-sellout feminism. Her early resume—Peace Corps in the early '60s, then a Syracuse public affairs doctoral degree—conjures an era when battalions of promising debate team captains were groomed to be Great Society bureaucrats, but then The Seventies intervened. Somehow as a rookie Columbia Teachers College professor in 1975 she became the only non-banker appointed to the nine-member Municipal Assistance Corporation, where she befriended the financier Felix Rohatyn, and from then on, in a series of ever more important jobs she perpetually astounded with her apparent fundraising prowess. She befriended Hillary in the '70s at the Children's Defense Fund; in 1985 she helped found EMILY's List with IBM heiress Ellen Malcolm; she was appointed health and human services secretary, when the running Beltway "joke" held that HHS stands for "Hillary's Health Service"; and she reversed the FDA's importation ban on RU-486 two days after the inauguration and dispatched Felix Rohatyn to Germany to convince Hoechst to transfer the drug's American patent rights to the Population Council "on behalf of American women." She survived the Hillarycare personnel bloodbath to preside over the scheme to eradicate the Temporary Assistance for Needy Families program in 1995—eliminating vital assistance that might have made it possible for some women *not* to choose abortion, if they preferred—and became Clinton's longest serving cabinet member in 2000, when the FDA she oversaw finally approved RU-486 after an epic saga of backroom money-wrangling.

It took a year and a half for the Population Council to ready itself to accept the patent and another year to appoint a business director to solicit investors to bankroll the clinical trials. After that, it took another three years to get rid of the person they'd initially appointed to that position, when he turned out to be a disbarred felon.[6] The project hit yet another snag in 1998 when one of its deepest-pocketed investors called to say that his hedge fund was about to collapse, rendering him "broke" and unable to cough up the eight-figure sum he had pledged to finance the tests and pay the Chinese factory contracted to produce the pills. This turned out to be a white lie aimed purely at shielding the financier's assets in case he failed to secure the billion-dollar bailout required to keep him and his partners out of bankruptcy court—don't worry, the Fed intervened just in time, and neither Greg Hawkins nor any other principals of Long Term Capital Management were forced to do any such thing—but sorting it out consumed many billable hours and cannot have possibly served to make the drug more affordable or accessible. Meanwhile Republicans were sweeping Congress, and drafting articles of impeachment, and negotiating with Hoechst to acquire for themselves the American rights to once-lucrative drugs battered by pro-life boycotts (like the hypertension treatment Altace, which made a veritable overnight billionaire of the Nashville pharmacist and evangelical Christian who acquired it in 1996.)[7] In short, as Team Clinton controversies tend to do, this one allowed a few characters of varying savoriness and party affiliation to make a very modest return on their investment and the status quo to remain unchanged.

None of this hurt the abortion lobby. Had pill abortion taken off as an affordable option, it would have diminished the abortion lobby's importance within the Democratic Party. But I doubt it was a conspiracy—the pill probably failed more due to the incompetence and shortsightedness of the major players than to some cynical grand design.

Still, the whole episode should make us wonder: maybe the abortion lobby wasn't just part of neoliberalism; maybe it *was* neoliberalism in action, all along.

It hasn't been easy to write this essay. I have a four-month-old son now and he truly hates it when I try to write anything. I had to send his babysitter home three hours early this evening because he was just too fucking impossible. But hey: he's amazing. A major reason I started trying to write this in the first place is my long-standing belief that "reproductive choice" ought to truly mean *choice*. What I couldn't have quite articulated before he came is the full gambit of that meaning, that depriving people of the opportunity to have kids is like depriving them of the opportunity to fall in love.

The right to choose to abort a fetus is critical, as is the ability to effect that choice in real life, so it's great that Hillary Clinton wants to repeal the Hyde Amendment. But without welfare, single-payer health care, a minimum wage of at least $15—all policies she staunchly opposes—many people have to forgo babies they'd really love to have. That's not really choice.

It seems ill-conceived to have tethered feminism to such a narrow issue as abortion. Yet it makes sense from an insular Beltway fundraising perspective to focus on an issue that makes no demands—the opposite, really—of the oligarch class; this is probably a big reason why EMILY's List has never dabbled in backing universal pre-K or paid maternity leave; a major reason "reproductive choice" has such a narrow and negative definition in the American political discourse.

The thing is, an abortion is *by definition* a story you want to forget, not repeat and relive. And for the same reason abortion pills will never be the blockbuster moneymakers heartburn medications are, abortion is a consummately foolish thing to attempt to build a political movement around. It happens once or twice in a woman's lifetime.

Kids, on the other hand, are with you forever. A more promising movement—one that goes against everything Hillary Clinton stands for—might take that to heart.

PART II: HILLARY ABROAD

TEN

Hillary Screws Sex Workers

Margaret Corvid

I n US politics, debate on the nature of sex work and the laws around it is rare, in contrast to the United Kingdom, where sex workers rights advocates—and active sex workers—speak for decriminalization at the highest levels of politics and in the national press.

The English Collective of Prostitutes has developed a pledge supporting the decriminalization of sex work that politicians and groups can sign. It has gained support among members of parliament across party lines; its most prominent and vocal supporters are socialist Labour leader Jeremy Corbyn and his shadow chancellor, John McDonnell MP. While Labour is divided, the Liberal Democrats and Greens officially support decriminalization. But in the US, "decriminalizing sex work" almost never appears in those perennial lists of signal issues—gun control, abortion, taxes, immigration, and so on—that newspapers put to candidates each election season.

In the United States, laws surrounding sex work are determined at the state level, so the legal status of sex work is rarely an issue in a presidential campaign. There's also an even more important cultural reason for the silence. In the US, where selling sex is illegal in every state except Nevada, a politician advocating clearly for the decriminalization of sex work would risk losing support, because in the American political imagination, a sex worker can only be either a criminal or a victim. "If any politician were to speak out on behalf of sex workers, it would be political suicide," says Bella Robinson, the Rhode Island director of the sex worker rights activist group COYOTE. "The trafficking narrative has misled politicians and prostitution has always been highly stigmatized in the US. It is easier for them to keep on course with policies that are failing and the outright lie to the media about women being rescued, when women are being arrested and not even offered any real services, like housing," she says.

Still, a small-city Nevada paper, in a county with its own legalized, regulated sex work, did ask Hillary Clinton a straight question about sex work eight years ago, during her first presidential campaign. She offered her clearest opinion on sex work to date:

> I do not approve of legalized prostitution or any kind of prostitution. It is something that I personally believe is demeaning to women. I have worked against it and I have certainly taken a very strong stand against what happens in many parts of the world where young girls and women are forced into prostitution against their wills. I understand Nevada has a regulated system and it is within the authority of the state. So that is not a federal issue that we will have any role to play in when I am president. But I would obviously speak out against prostitution and try to persuade women that it is not—even in a regulated system—necessarily a good way to try to make a living. Let's try to find other jobs that

can be there for women who are looking for a good way to support themselves and their families.[1]

Clinton has rarely spoken so bluntly as she did in 2007 about voluntary sex work. Like many other politicians, she has tended to conflate voluntary and coerced sex work under the label of trafficking. And trafficking is an issue that Hillary Clinton has made central to her career. In doing so, she has, despite her oft-touted feminism, pursued policies that hurt girls and women.

Anyone who loves justice opposes people being forced to do sex work as a matter of basic principle. That's why in today's media landscape, "fighting traffickers" or "combating modern slavery" is as uncontroversially lauded as fighting cancer, with an extra pop feminist, multiculturalist, global, soft-power fillip. The notion of trafficking itself, however, is deeply problematic. As Laura Agustín explains in her book *Sex at the Margins*, "trafficking" is a word created expressly to attach a criminal label to migratory and economic behavior. There's no scientific standard for the term:

> Some projects attempting to quantify victims count all migrants who sell sex, others consider anyone who agrees to denounce a "trafficker" according to local law, others count everyone who gives money to a boyfriend, and yet others include all illegal sex workers. Victims may be tallied only in countries of origin or only in destinations or in both; studies may include transit countries or not. Attempts at quantification are made more unreliable, moreover, because most segments of the sex sector are not recognized by governments, which means there can be no proper counting of "sex workers," as a category, either.[2]

Far from liberating slaves, global efforts to combat the shibboleth of trafficking, efforts that work in concert with criminalization, mean that sex workers face violence, violation, stigma, poverty, and death at the hands of police, rescuers, or predators pretending to be clients. In the United States, recent campaigns against trafficking conducted by federal law enforcement have overwhelmingly caught independent sex workers and undocumented immigrants who were performing sex work voluntarily. Disproportionately affecting the most marginalized sex workers, including people of color, trans people, single parents, and those who have previous criminal convictions, these crusades against trafficking leave sex workers even less able to seek help from law enforcement when they actually need it, for instance if they face coercion or wish to report underage sex work.

"Together we must implement a comprehensive approach that both confronts criminals and cares for survivors," exhorted Secretary Clinton in an address to a 2009 Organization for Security and Co-operation in Europe conference on preventing trafficking.[3] Though it sounds progressive on its surface, this statement's conflation of the complex issues around work and migration into only two categories—criminals and survivors—tells us a great deal about Clinton's views on sex work.

In her work as a first lady, as a New York senator, and as secretary of state, Clinton has campaigned vocally against trafficking and has supported organizations that have been shown to imprison and abuse sex workers. Robin D., writing at the first-class sex worker blog Tits and Sass, summed up her role: "Hillary Clinton is not responsible for the terrible policies of the Bush Administration, but she is responsible for following in lock-step with those policies during her tenure as Secretary of State under the Obama Administration."[4]

The State Department manages the Trafficking in Persons (TIP) office, which ranks countries based on performance in this area in an annual report. When Cambodia criminalized prostitution, setting up diversion programs that threw sex workers into rehabilitation centers where they were subject to rape and violence, Clinton's State awarded it an improved ranking. (Countries can face sanctions and

lose various kinds of aid from the United States if their TIP rank-
ings are poor.) Criminalization led to rescue organizations privately
funded largely by Christian organizations participating in brutal
street and brothel raids alongside Cambodian police. Clinton
maintained a close relationship with AFESIP, the Cambodian
rescue organization run by Somaly Mam, who was later discred-
ited by Newsweek reporters, as well as by a law firm hired by her
own foundation, for fabricating her own story and the stories of
the women and girls being helped by her organization. (Mam later
insisted that she "didn't lie.")[5] Brought into the spotlight, AFESIP
was also revealed to be holding women and girls against their
will.[6] Clinton served on the global advisory board of the Somaly
Mam Foundation, which funded rescue groups worldwide until its
closure in 2014.[7]

The TIP report is only one of the tactics the State Department
uses to further criminalize sex work. State also administers many
millions of dollars in global aid and development funds. In a lit-
tle-noticed 2008 legislative codicil to its massive global anti-AIDS
funding campaign, the US Agency for International Development
denied funding to any organization that did not explicitly oppose
prostitution;[8] this was only overturned by the Supreme Court in
2014, by a case brought by organizations that refused to disavow
the sex workers that they helped.

Global public health bodies and human rights organizations,
from Amnesty International to UNAIDS to Human Rights Watch,
have condemned the criminalization of sex work in all its forms.
Amnesty International's June 2015 policy statement in support of
full decriminalization has sparked a furious worldwide debate, in
which the lives of sex workers under criminalization—plagued with
violence, stigma, poverty, and marginalization—have come into the
foreground. Sex workers' voices are being heard in the national press
and broadcast media, in countries like Britain, Ireland, Australia,
France, Spain, and even the Ukraine.

But in the United States, there is no national debate where sex workers have a place at the table. By helping to shape the American narrative around sex work, obscuring us as either criminals or survivors, Hillary Clinton has helped to keep us invisible, and she must like it that way.

Clinton's State Department funded American rescue industry groups, largely Christian and mostly led by white men, who lead rescue operations abroad and work with law enforcement at home. These groups rarely offer concrete services, like housing, medical care or food aid, to the sex workers they "rescue." Polaris Project, one group funded by State, runs a trafficking hotline and purports to help victims. But when Bella Robinson tried to contact Polaris to find assistance for a coerced sex worker, she found little practical help. "The US is funding trafficking NGOs at 686 million a year and most of the money goes to 'creating awareness on sex trafficking,' and the rest [of the money funneled into those organizations] goes to pay their board members, many who make six-figure salaries," says Robinson.[9] "When I called Polaris they said they don't investigate anything, all they do is relay the tips to local police. I said, 'Can't people just dial 911 and we can save the 3 to 7 million a year you get in federal funding?' They admitted they do not have any direct services, so all they do is refer victims to public shelters. A person can dial 211 and get a list of the same fake services."[10]

We cannot expect a President Clinton to change her mind on the nature of sex work, even if she is confronted with the impartial research of Amnesty International or the bare statistics on the failure and unconstitutional inhumanity of Operation Cross Country. She is not someone who lacks facts. (Of course, Hillary Clinton is a product of her environment: in an American political and public atmosphere so dominated by the religious right, there will be no Jeremy Corbyn for the American sex worker.) She has swallowed the false paradigm of rescue whole; it is an integral part of who she is and the system of state power that she represents. It is unsurprising that a candidate who believes that sex workers are victims to be rescued, criminals to be prosecuted, or survivors to be purified also believes that the solution to the humanitarian crisis of Syrian refugees in 2015—the plan for their rescue—should be to bomb their country into dust.

There will always be a few harboring illusions about her, but the only sex workers publicly supporting Clinton are the Hookers for Hillary—sex workers touring at Dennis Hof's legal Nevada Moonlite Bunny Ranch,[8] who say they support Hillary because she's for affordable health care, and Obama's Affordable Care Act has let the independent contractors legally selling sex at the ranch purchase health insurance. But the "bunnies'" endorsement page says nothing about the broader decriminalization of sex work or Clinton's position on the matter.

Because the Hookers for Hillary live and work in Nevada, where sex work is legal in some counties, they enjoy a freedom that their candidate opposes. The best way to ensure safe, legal, and ethical sex work is decriminalization, as in New Zealand, where sex work is lightly regulated, and sex workers enjoy the same protections for health, safety, and the right to organize as workers in other industries do. But how can we achieve this status in the rest of the United States, if not through electoral politics?

Many sex workers believe the answer lies in the courts. Tara Burns writes:

> Like we saw recently in the Supreme Court decision to allow gay marriage, the courts are where minority peoples most often see our rights affirmed. The Supreme Court's job is not to act as a moral arbitrator or to interpret the will of the people. It's to interpret the law, beginning with the constitution. LGBT [lesbian, gay, bisexual, and transgender] people were being denied their constitutional right to equal protection under the law ... Now LGBT people are

not being denied their right to equal protection under marriage laws. Well, except for by Kim Davis. Sex workers and our clients are currently being denied access to several of our constitutional rights. These include privacy, equal protection under the law, and due process. What is needed is a finding by the federal Supreme Court (and/or each state's Supreme Court—that's how it was done in Rhode Island) that states are violating our constitutional rights with the prostitution laws.[9]

The Erotic Service Provider Legal, Educational and Research Project, a sex worker group in California, is currently waging a lawsuit to make this approach a reality. Their case, which sex workers and supporters have supported financially, challenges the criminalization of sex work on the basis that it violates the constitutional right of freedom of association.

Legal challenges like these (and not electoral politics) are the best chance for sex workers in the United States to win the right to work in safety and peace. But it's still important for feminists to oppose candidates who oppose justice for this embattled group of (mostly women) workers. And Hillary Clinton is such a candidate. I understand the yearning for a woman president. I understand the hope that Clinton could somehow make a real difference toward liberation. But without a frank reevaluation of her position on sex work, it is impossible for her to call herself a feminist as that term is understood today.

ELEVEN

Hillary Does Honduras

Belén Fernández

Legend has it that the name "Honduras" derives from Christopher Columbus's expression of relief, in 1502, at averting a nautical demise off the Central American coast. "*Gracias a Dios que hemos salido de estas honduras,*" he is reported to have exclaimed. "Thank God we've gotten out of these depths."

More than 500 years later, Honduras has sunk to new depths, particularly following the June 2009 coup d'état against President Manuel Zelaya, which enabled the small nation to solidify its position as the homicide capital of the world. The success of the coup was thanks in no small part to another imperial emissary, this one by the name of Hillary Rodham Clinton.

In the inaugural year of Barack Obama's presidency and Clinton's secretary of state-hood, many inhabitants of the globe still clung to the hope that the new multiracial team might oversee a departure from business as usual in US foreign policy. At the very least, the thinking went, the shameless sociopathy of the previous administration would be turned down a notch.

But even before Obama had a chance to carve out a name for himself as a drone-happy serial killer in the Middle East, the US made it clear that it was not going to play benign hegemon in its Latin American backyard. In some cases, it would pursue the Cold War tradition of extending support to repressive regional leaders—albeit in subtler fashion than in the good old days of dictators and death squads.

Home to the US airbase of Soto Cano and affectionately dubbed the "U.S.S. Honduras" in the 1980s on account of its role as a launchpad for Contra attacks against neighboring Nicaragua, Honduras's geostrategic importance has effectively condemned it to a contemporary history of rule by an oligarchic elite with sycophantic tendencies toward the gringos. When Zelaya began emitting slightly left-leaning noises—raising the urban and rural monthly minimum wages to $290 and $213, respectively—he was rendered persona non grata in the eyes of the oligarchs and their American buddies. After all, the attention Zelaya was recklessly paying laborers most certainly amounted to a slippery slope in the direction of a communist apocalypse.

The last straw arrived in the form of a nonbinding public opinion survey Zelaya had scheduled for June 28, in which the Honduran citizenry were to be asked the following question: Are you in favor of installing an extra ballot box at upcoming elections in order to conduct a vote on whether to convene a constituent assembly to tweak the national constitution? The constitution had for years served the interests of the rich minority at the expense of the general population.

The Honduran elites interpreted the survey project as confirmation that Honduras had become Venezuela, and Zelaya was accused of endeavoring to retain his hold on the presidency in violation of Article 239 of the constitution, which limited leaders to a single four-year stint. Never mind that the outcome of the survey would have had no bearing whatsoever on Zelaya's ineligibility to run in the next elections—or that, in response to the president's imagined transgression, the Honduran military promptly violated Article 102 of the constitution prohibiting the forced expatriation of any Honduran citizen.

In the predawn hours of June 28, the armed forces descended upon Zelaya's residence in the Honduran capital of Tegucigalpa and carted the pajama-clad leader off to Costa Rica. The following day, Obama denounced the event as a "coup" that was "not legal," but failed to deem it a "military coup," which would have triggered an immediate cutoff of US military and other aid to the country.

Enter Hillary Clinton, who declined to go so far as to even apply the C-word, announcing instead that "we are withholding any formal legal determination."[1] Indeed, one should never jump to conclusions about the proper terminology to use when a military ousts an elected president. Why not call it a pajama party?

We can safely assume that, had the very same act been perpe-trated against a pal of the US, Clinton would have wasted no time in issuing a formal legal determination.

Not all tentacles of the State Department shared Clinton's bewil-derment at what had transpired in Honduras or her commitment to an open-ended contemplation of its nature. When I visited the US embassy in Tegucigalpa in August 2009, for example, there were some serious slip-ups with regard to the official line. Deputy Mission Chief Simon Henshaw accidentally described Zelaya's ouster as a "military coup." US ambassador to Honduras Hugo Llorens then declared it a "clear-cut case of a coup" and finally a "whatever you call it."[2]

There was also some confusion about certain Honduras-bound funds from the Millennium Challenge Corporation (MCC), a self-described "independent US foreign aid agency," that were sup-posedly suspended pending the official verdict on the whatever you call it. Llorens's explanation for why millions of MCC dollars continued to flow into the country was that they were already "in the pipeline." The chair of the board of directors of the "independent" agency was none other than Clinton herself.

State Department press briefings on Honduras were also a regular source of tragicomedy. A July 1 teleconference briefing with "Senior Administration Official One" and "Senior Administration Official Two" featured award-winning performances in ambiguity:

> QUESTION: And so this is properly classified as a military coup?
> SENIOR ADMINISTRATION OFFICIAL ONE: Well, I mean, it's a *golpe de estado* [In Spanish: coup d'état]. The military moved against the president; they removed him from his home and they expelled him from a country, so the military participated in a coup. However, the transfer of leadership was not a military action. The transfer of leadership was done by the Honduran congress, and therefore the coup, while it had a military component, it has a larger—it is a larger event.

Meanwhile, Clinton was working away behind the scenes to ensure that a reinstatement of Zelaya was avoided at all costs. We know this because she tells us so in her memoir *Hard Choices*, published in 2014, in which she categorizes Zelaya as "a throwback to the caricature of a Central American strongman, with his white cowboy hat, dark black mustache, and fondness for Hugo Chávez and Fidel Castro."[3]

As Clinton tells it, in the days following Zelaya's removal she conferred with her hemispheric counterparts, including Mexico's secretary of foreign affairs: "We strategized on a plan to restore order in Honduras and ensure that free and fair elections could be held quickly and legitimately, which would render the question of Zelaya moot and give the Honduran people a chance to choose their own future."[4] Among the various problems with this reasoning, of course, is that the Honduran people had already chosen Zelaya to serve out his four-year term—a choice that Clinton's strategy overrode. Furthermore, elections held under an illegitimate, coup-installed regime are by definition neither free nor fair. Interestingly, the whole section of Clinton's book focusing on the rendering moot of the Zelaya question has disappeared from the paperback edition, released in 2015.

Leaked emails reveal that Clinton had suggested using her old law school friend Lanny Davis as a back-channel liaison to the interim putschist president Roberto Micheletti, whose antics in office included declaring it a "gift from god" when rabid right-wing US congresswoman Ileana Ros-Lehtinen visited Tegucigalpa to sing the praises of the coup. Davis, a former special counsel to Bill Clinton who helped organize a Ready for Hillary fundraiser in the DC suburbs in December 2014, is described in a blog post at the *Intercept* as a "high-powered 'crisis communications' adviser to a variety of people and organizations facing negative attention in the media, from scandal-plagued for-profit college companies to African dictators."[5]

In the aftermath of the coup against Zelaya, Davis was hired by the Latin American Business Council of Honduras to shill for the coup regime and whitewash the coup itself on Capitol Hill. In addition to lobbying activities, he authored an op-ed for the *Wall Street Journal*. Claiming that Zelaya had "violated the [Honduran] constitution by pushing for a vote that would have allowed him to extend his time in office"—which we've already established was not even within the realm of potential outcomes of his proposed survey—Davis went on to allege that Zelaya's overarching goal had been to "declare himself president ad infinitum."[6]

These unhinged musings fit right in on that newspapers opinion page. Consider the presence on the *Journal*'s editorial board of Mary Anastasia O'Grady, a columnist on Latin America and a fierce opponent of anything less than fanatically right-wing. O'Grady's own warped analysis of the post-coup dynamics can be boiled down to the following two points:

In cahoots with Chávez, Castro, and other like-minded souls, Hillary Clinton malevolently agitated to have Zelaya restored to power, in defiance of Honduran democracy.
Hugo Llorens also defied Honduran democracy, and is therefore deserving of a diplomatic post in Cuba.

Despite Clinton's best efforts, however, this international communist plot fell through, Zelaya remained overthrown, and elections were held on November 29, 2009. A farcical and fraudulent spectacle—boycotted by "all major international observers," historian Dana Frank notes in a *New York Times* op-ed, "except for the National Democratic Institute and the International Republican Institute, which are financed by the United States"—the election produced the illegitimate presidency of Porfirio Lobo.[7]

The months of hemming and hawing by the State Department over the extent to which the Honduran coup was or was not coup-like had allowed the country's reactionary forces to reconsolidate their power and return with a vengeance. Gone were the days in which a Honduran president would even consider, as Zelaya had, asking rural communities how they felt about being subjected to harmful foreign corporate mining practices. Peasant farmers in the northeastern Aguán Valley whom Zelaya had pledged to assist in recuperating their land rights were now left at the mercy of Honduran security forces and hit men often working on behalf of the (now deceased) Miguel Facussé, the country's largest landowner.

In his 2014 documentary *Resistencia: The Fight for the Aguán Valley*, Canadian videojournalist Jesse Freeston observes that "since the coup, the US government has increased military aid to Honduras to its highest levels in history, with the stated purpose of fighting drug trafficking." Yet, according to a cable from the US embassy in

Honduras published by Wikileaks in 2011, the State Department has known since 2004 that planes carrying cocaine from Colombia land directly on airstrips at Miguel Facussé's plantations.

Unlike many Honduran citizens and Latin American governments, the US promptly recognized the 2009 elections, with Obama jubilantly proclaiming less than two years later a "restoration of democratic practices [in Honduras] and a commitment to reconciliation" on the part of the Lobo regime.[8] But while the American political class continues to perfect its talent for perverting beyond recognition stock vocabulary words like "democracy" and "human rights," other observers tell it like it is.

In her 2012 *New York Times* piece, titled "In Honduras, a Mess Made in the U.S.," Dana Frank details the nation's post-coup descent "deeper into a human rights and security abyss [that] is in good part the State Department's making." Thanks largely to Washington's conciliatory approach to the events in Honduras, corruption and impunity became essentially institutionalized with people perishing left and right, many at the hands of state security forces funded by the United States. This was a trend that continued seamlessly from the coup government's tenure into the democratic renaissance supposedly presided over by Lobo.

To pick just a few casualties from the many, Honduran teenager Isis Obed Murillo was shot in the head by the military while attending a gathering at Tegucigalpa's Toncontín airport on July 5, 2009, intended as a welcome-home ceremony for the recently deposed Zelaya, who was then attempting a return to the country by plane. (His landing was thwarted.) *La Prensa*, one of the top Honduran dailies, took the liberty of photoshopping the blood out of Murillo's photograph to imply that he had fainted, not been murdered. Later that month, secondary school teacher Roger Vallejo was also shot in the head by Honduran police while participating in an anti-coup demonstration. *El Heraldo*, another prominent newspaper, indignantly explained (July 31, 2009) that "he had abandoned his classroom in order to go out and protest in the streets."

Fast forward to March 2011, shortly before Obama detected a "restoration of democratic practices" in Honduras, when fifty-nine-year-old schoolteacher Ilse Velásquez was struck in the head by a tear gas canister fired by police at a march against the privatization of public education. She was then run over by a press vehicle and died. The moral of the story, according to *El Heraldo*: counterfeit dollars arriving from Venezuela were financing Nicaraguan-infiltrated teacher protests.[9] The moral of the story, according to the Human Rights and Labor Attaché at the US embassy in Tegucigalpa: there were "thugs" among the nation's educators, and "most Hondurans believe[d] the teachers should return to their classrooms."[10] Velásquez, it bears mentioning, happened to be the sister of a teacher who was disappeared in 1981 by Battalion 3-16, a CIA-trained elite death squad.

Regarding the latest round of US-backed oppression in Honduras, Mark Weisbrot of the Center for Economic and Policy Research in Washington, DC, outlines in a 2014 op-ed for Al Jazeera America the dark reality that unfolded following the coup:

> The homicide rate in Honduras, already the highest in the world, increased by 50 percent from 2008 to 2011; political repression, the murder of opposition political candidates, peasant organizers and [lesbian, gay, bisexual, and transgender] activists increased and continue to this day. Femicides skyrocketed. The violence and insecurity were exacerbated by a generalized institutional collapse. Drug-related violence has worsened amid allegations of rampant corruption in Honduras' police and government. While the gangs are responsible for much of the violence, Honduran security forces have engaged in a wave of killings and other human rights crimes with impunity.[11]

To be sure, femicide does not fit easily into the marketed image of Clinton as an ardent champion of women's rights. Among persons who would, were they still breathing, presumably take issue with Clinton's enthusiasm over the prospect of "restor[ing] democratic and constitutional order" in Honduras via elections is Soad Ham, a thirteen-year-old student leader in Tegucigalpa at the time of her death. After helping to organize demonstrations against the Honduran education minister's meddling with class schedules, which would have elongated the school day and endangered the safety of students departing from school in the evening, she was found tortured and killed in March 2015, her remains in a plastic bag.

Obviously, it's not only in Honduras that Clinton's projected feminist orientation fails to cohere with reality. Her previous support for the war on Iraq and her continuing support for crimes regularly perpetrated by the state of Israel also reek of hypocrisy, as both missions have proven highly destructive to the lives of women and girls, not to mention their male counterparts. According to the UN's investigation into the Israeli military's fifty-one-day assault on the Gaza Strip in 2014 (dubbed Operation Protective Edge), 2,251 Palestinians were killed during the affair, most of them civilians; 299 were women, and 551 were children. In an interview with *The Atlantic*'s Jeffrey Goldberg, Clinton argued, "I think Israel did what it had to do," regurgitating that preferred line of Israeli and US politicians alike: "Israel has a right to defend itself."[12]

Nor do women benefit from Clinton-sanctioned economic belligerence. In an essay for *Jacobin* magazine, Kevin Young and Diana C. Sierra Becerra note that, in Haiti, "Clinton and her husband have relentlessly promoted the sweatshop model of production since the 1990s."[13] The authors continue: "WikiLeaks documents show that in 2009 her State Department collaborated with subcontractors for Hanes, Levi's, and Fruit of the Loom to oppose a minimum-wage increase for Haitian workers." According to a measure passed unanimously by the Haitian Parliament in June 2009, the minimum wage for Haitian assembly zone workers was to be raised to a whopping 62 cents per hour, or about $5 per day—a move that apparently just couldn't be tolerated by Haiti's friendly neighbor to the north. Hey, US corporations need to eat, too!

On the Honduran front, Frank contends that the Clinton State Department's die-hard support for the Lobo administration was in part evidence of its having "caved in to the Cuban-American constituency" of Ileana Ros-Lehtinen, then the chairwoman of the House Foreign Affairs Committee. Ros-Lehtinen and friends, Frank writes, had "been ferocious about Honduras as a first domino with which to push back against the line of center-left and leftist governments that [had] won elections in Latin America in the past fifteen years."[14]

Weisbrot agrees that "Clinton's embrace of the far-right narrative in the Honduran episode" was part of a "political calculation" that goes something like this:

> There is little risk of losing votes for admitting her role in making most of the hemisphere's governments disgusted with the United States. On the other side of the equation, there are influential interest groups and significant campaign money to be raised from the right-wing Latin American lobby, including Floridian Cuban-Americans and their political fundraisers.[15]

But while there is certainly something to be said about the influence of fearmongering hysterics by the American right, the fact remains that there is a bipartisan commitment to neoliberalizing the world and making life hell for many a global have-not. The "freedom" that the US so loftily purports to spread translates into freedom for capital, not for human beings; it's therefore not surprising that one of the crowning achievements of the repressive Lobo government was an economic conference—i.e., a shameless spectacle of investor ass-kissing—titled "Honduras Is Open for Business." Nor is it surprising, perhaps, with the country now firmly in the hands of the ultra-right, that the Honduran Supreme Court has done away with the very constitutional article on term limits that was invoked to justify the overthrow of Zelaya.

When contemplating the US political landscape, it sometimes seems that the difference between the Republicans and the Democrats is that the former are unabashedly odious while the latter do a better job of concealing their odiousness. But Clinton can't even rock the disguise.

TWELVE

Pink-Slipping Hillary

Medea Benjamin

I n March 2003, just before the US invasion of Iraq, about one hundred CODEPINK women dressed in pink slips weaved in and out of congressional offices demanding to meet with representatives. Those representatives who pledged to oppose going to war with Iraq were given hugs and pink badges of courage; those hell-bent on taking the US to war were given pink slips emblazoned with the words "YOU'RE FIRED."

When we got to Hillary Clinton's office, we sat down and refused to leave until we had a meeting with the senator. Within an hour, Clinton appeared. "I like pink tulips around this time of the year; they kind of remind ya that there may be a spring," she began, looking out at the rows of women in pink. "Well, you guys look like a big bunch of big tulips!"

It got even more awkward after that. Having just returned from Iraq, I relayed that the weapons inspectors in Baghdad told us there was no danger of weapons of mass destruction and that the Iraqi women we met were terrified about the pending war and desperate to stop it. "I admire your willingness to speak out on behalf of the women and children of Iraq," Clinton replied, "but there is a very easy way to prevent anyone from being put into harm's way and that is for Saddam Hussein to disarm and I have absolutely no belief that he will."

We thought the easiest way to prevent harming women, children and other living things in Iraq was to stop a war of aggression, a war over weapons of mass destruction that UN inspectors on the ground couldn't find—which were, in fact, never found because they didn't exist. Clinton, however, was steadfast in her commitment to war: She said it was our responsibility to disarm Saddam Hussein and even defended George W. Bush's unilateralism, citing her husband's go-it-alone intervention in Kosovo.

Disgusted, CODEPINK cofounder Jodie Evans tore off her pink slip and handed it to Clinton, saying that her support for Bush's invasion would lead to the death of many innocent people. Making the bogus connection between the September 11, 2001, attacks and Saddam Hussein, Clinton stormed out, saying, "I am the senator from New York. I will never put my people's security at risk."

But that's just what she did, by supporting the Iraq war, draining our nation of over a trillion dollars that could have been used for supporting women and children here at home, which could have instead been rerouted to the social programs that have been systematically defunded over the last few decades of Clinton's own political career, and ultimately snuffing out the lives of thousands of US soldiers—for absolutely no just cause.

If Clinton supported the Iraq war because she thought it politically expedient, she came to regret her stance when the war turned sour and Senator Barack Obama surged forward as the candidate opposed to that war.

But Clinton didn't learn the main lesson from Iraq—to seek nonviolent ways to solve conflicts.

Indeed, when the Arab Spring came to Libya in 2010, Clinton was the Obama administration's most forceful advocate for toppling Muammar Gaddafi. She even out-hawked Robert Gates, the defense secretary first appointed by George W. Bush, who was less than enthusiastic about going to war. Gates was reluctant to get bogged down in another Arab country, insisting that vital US interests were not at stake, but Clinton nevertheless favored intervention.

When Libyan rebels carried out an extrajudicial execution of their country's former dictator, Clinton's response was sociopathic: "We came, we saw, he died," she laughed. That sent a message that the US would look the other way at crimes committed by allies against its official enemies.

In a weird bit of rough justice, the political grief Clinton has suffered over the September 11, 2012, attack on a US diplomatic outpost in Benghazi that killed four Americans might never have occurred had Clinton not supported the US intervention in Libya's civil war. While Republicans have focused relentlessly on the terrible deaths of the US diplomats, the larger disaster is the ensuing chaos that left Libya without a functioning government, overrun by feuding warlords and extremist militants. In 2015, the suffering of desperate refugees who flee civil unrest—many of whom drown in the Mediterranean Sea—is a direct consequence of that disastrous operation.

Libya was part of a pattern for Clinton. On Afghanistan, she advocated a repeat of the surge in Iraq. When the top US commander in Kabul, General Stanley McChrystal, asked Obama for 40,000 more troops to fight the Taliban in mid-2009, several top officials—including Vice President Joe Biden—objected, insisting that the public had lost patience with a conflict that had already dragged on too long. But Clinton backed McChrystal and wound up favoring even more surge troops than Defense Secretary Gates did. Obama ultimately sent another 30,000 American soldiers to Afghanistan.

Clinton's State Department also provided cover for the expansion of the not-so-covert drone wars in Pakistan and Yemen. Clinton's top legal adviser, Harold Koh, exploited his pregovernment reputation as an advocate for human rights to declare in a 2010 speech that the government had the right not only to detain people without any charges at Guantanamo Bay but also to kill them with unmanned aerial vehicles anywhere in the world.[1]

When it came to Syria, Obama's top diplomat was a forceful advocate for military intervention in that nation's civil war. When Obama threatened air strikes in 2013 to punish the Assad regime's use of chemical weapons, Clinton publicly supported him, ignoring polls showing that more than 70 percent of Americans opposed military action.[2] She described the planned US attack on Syria as a "limited strike to uphold a crucial global norm," although one of the clearest global norms under the UN Charter is that a country should not attack another country except in self-defense.

Clinton advocated arming Syrian rebels long before the Obama administration agreed to do so. In 2012, she allied with CIA director David Petraeus to promote a US-supplied-and-trained proxy army in Syria. As a US Army general, Petraeus spent enormous amounts of money training Iraqi and Afghan soldiers with little success, but that did not deter him and Clinton from seeking a similar project in Syria. Together, they campaigned for more direct and aggressive US support for the rebels, a plan supported by leading Republicans like John McCain and Lindsey Graham. But few in the White House agreed, arguing that it would be difficult to appropriately vet fighters and ensure that weapons didn't fall into the hands of extremists.

Clinton was disappointed when Obama rejected the proposal, but a similar plan for the US to "vet and train moderate rebels" at a starting cost of $500 million was later approved. Some of the trained rebels were quickly routed and captured; others, more concerned with toppling Assad than fighting Islamic State in Iraq and Syria (ISIL), defected to the al-Qaeda affiliate al-Nusra. In September

2015, commander of US Central Command General Lloyd Austin told an incredulous Senate Armed Services Committee that the $500 million effort to train Syrian forces has resulted in a mere four or five fighters actively battling ISIL. Undeterred, Clinton said that as commander-in-chief, she would dramatically escalate the program.

In October 2015, Clinton broke with the Obama White House on Syria by calling for the creation of a no-fly zone "to try to stop the carnage on the ground and from the air, to try to provide some way to take stock of what's happening, to try to stem the flow of refugees," she said in a TV interview on the campaign trail.[3]

While the Obama White House approved limited air strikes against ISIL, it has resisted creating a no-fly zone on the grounds that effective enforcement to prevent Assad's planes from flying would require large amounts of US resources and could pull the military further into an unpredictable conflict.

Clinton's position is at odds not only with President Obama but also with Bernie Sanders, who, at this writing, is her main rival for the Democratic presidential nomination. Sanders has warned that a unilateral US no-fly zone in Syria could "get us more deeply involved in that horrible civil war and lead to a never-ending US entanglement in that region," potentially making a complex and dangerous situation in Syria even worse.[4]

Clinton did come out in support of President Obama's nuclear deal with Iran, but even that position comes with a heavy load of bellicose baggage. Back in April 2008 she warned that the US could "totally obliterate" Iran in retaliation for a nuclear attack on Israel—prompting Obama to warn against "language that's reflective of George Bush."[5] In 2009, as secretary of state, she was adamant that the US keep open the option of attacking Iran over never-proven allegations it was seeking the nuclear weapons that Israel already has.[6] She opposed talk of a "containment" policy that would be an alternative to military action should negotiations with Tehran fail.

Even after the agreement was sealed, she struck a bullying tone: "I don't believe Iran is our partner in this agreement," Clinton insisted. "Iran is the subject of the agreement," adding that she would not hesitate to take military action if Iran attempts to obtain a nuclear weapon. "We should expect that Iran will want to test the next president. They will want to see how far they can bend the rules," she said in a September 2015 speech at the Brookings Institution. "That won't work if I'm in the White House."[7]

To bolster her tough stance, Clinton suggested deploying additional US forces to the Persian Gulf region and recommended that Congress close any gaps in the existing sanctions to punish Iran for any current or future instances of human rights abuses and support for terror.

It's true that the Iran nuclear agreement allowed for additional possible sanctions unrelated to Iran's nuclear program, but it also required parties to avoid action "inconsistent with the letter, spirit and intent" of the deal. Clinton's call for new sanctions violates the deal's intent.

On Israel, Clinton has positioned herself as more "pro-Israel" than President Obama. She vows to bring the two nations closer together, promising to invite the right-wing Israeli prime minister Benjamin Netanyahu to visit the White House within her first month in office. She has distanced herself from Obama's feud with Netanyahu over the prime minister's efforts to derail the Iran nuclear deal and his comments opposing the creation of a Palestinian state. Referring to Obama's policy toward Netanyahu, Clinton said that such "tough love" is counterproductive because it invites other countries to delegitimize Israel. Clinton promised the people of Israel that if she were president, "you'll never have to question whether we're with you. The United States will always be with you."[8]

Clinton has also voiced her opposition to the Palestinian-led nonviolent campaign against the Israeli government called BDS—boycott, divestment, and sanctions. In a letter to Jewish mega donor Haim Saban, she said BDS seeks to punish Israel and asked Saban's advice on "how leaders and communities across America can work together to counter BDS."[9]

As secretary of state, Clinton missed opportunity after opportunity to shine as the nation's top diplomat. In July 2010 she visited the Korean Demilitarized Zone with Defense Secretary Robert Gates to commemorate the sixtieth anniversary of the start of the Korean War. Standing at the site of the most militarized border in the world at a time of great tension between North and South Korea, she could have publicly recognized that the 1953 Armistice Agreement that ended the fighting on the Korean peninsula was supposed to be followed up a few months later by a peace treaty that would move toward reconciliation and that this had never happened. Clinton could have used this occasion to call for a peace treaty and a process of reconciliation between the two Koreas. Instead she claimed that the US military presence in Korea for decades had led to the current successful result, a statement hard to reconcile with sixty years of continuous hostilities.

As secretary of state, Clinton failed miserably in her attempt to "reset" the US relationship with Russia, and after leaving office, she has criticized the Obama administration for not doing more to contain Russia's presence in Ukraine since the 2014 annexation of Crimea. She put herself "in the category of people who wanted to do more in reaction to the annexation of Crimea," insisting that the Russian government's objective is "to stymie, to confront, to undermine American power whenever and wherever they can."[10]

It was only after Clinton resigned as secretary of state and was replaced by John Kerry that the agency moved away from being merely an appendage of the Pentagon to one that truly sought creative, diplomatic solutions to seemingly intractable conflicts. President Obama's two signature foreign policy achievements—the Iran deal and the groundbreaking opening with Cuba—came after Clinton left. These historic wins serve to highlight Clinton's miserable track record in the position.

*   *   *

When Clinton announced her second campaign for the presidency, she declared she was entering the race to be the champion for "everyday Americans." As a lawmaker and diplomat, however, Clinton has long championed military campaigns that have killed scores of "everyday" people abroad. There's no reason to believe that as commander-in-chief she'd be any less a warhawk than she was as the senator who backed George W. Bush's war in Iraq, or the secretary of state who encouraged Barack Obama to escalate the war in Afghanistan.

Clinton may well have been the administration's most vociferous advocate for military action. On at least three crucial issues—Afghanistan, Libya, and the bin Laden raid—she took a more aggressive line than Defense Secretary Gates, a Bush-appointed Republican.

Little wonder that Clinton has won the support of many pundits who continually agitate for war. "I feel comfortable with her on foreign policy," Robert Kagan, a co-founder of the neoconservative Project for the New American Century, told the *New York Times*. "If she pursues a policy which we think she will pursue," he said, "it's something that might have been called neocon, but clearly her supporters are not going to call it that; they are going to call it something else."[11]

Let's call it what it is: more of the interventionist policies that destroyed Iraq, destabilized Libya, showered Yemen with cluster bombs and drones, and legitimized repressive regimes from Israel to Honduras.

A Hillary Clinton presidency would symbolically break the glass ceiling for women in the United States, but it would be unlikely to break through the military-industrial complex that has been keeping our nation in a perpetual state of war—killing people around the world, plenty of them women and children.

THIRTEEN

Beyond Hillary: Toward Anti-racist, Anti-imperialist Feminisms

Zillah Eisenstein

As a feminist, I don't encourage or advocate misogyny toward Hillary Clinton. And of course I'd love to see a woman become president. I also feel that if, ultimately, your vote for Clinton is needed to prevent a Republican from taking this country back to the nineteenth century, you should by all means go ahead and vote for her. But let us not, in our acknowledgement of these obvious feminist practicalities, lose sight of our opposition to the sort of feminism that Hillary Clinton represents and the harm it causes: equal opportunity warmongering. Because it is only out of such opposition that a better feminism can grow and thrive, one committed to peace, anti-racism, and the well-being of the 99 percent.

Much has been said of Clinton's criticism of the Obama administration's Syria policy, which she has blamed for the growth of Islamic State of Iraq and Syria (ISIS). Obama has committed limited ground troops, but she still insists he needs to do more. Much less critical attention has been given to her unequivocal embrace of Prime Minister Benjamin Netanyahu and Israel's war in Gaza. Her stances as a candidate, her actions as secretary of state, and her record as a senator show that she condones a perpetual state of war.

Meanwhile, and poignantly, Palestinians stand in solidarity with blacks in Ferguson, Missouri, against apartheid and racist policies aimed at "disposable others" like themselves.[1] They indict the militarized and warlike policing that kills them as well as unarmed black teenagers like Michael Brown. Militarist police officers in the US receive their formal training as well as equipment in and from Israel, which sets the standard for high stakes security.[2]

Indeed, while most feminisms in the United States and abroad have over the last three decades become more complicated, more complex, and more intersectional, actively anti-racist and anti-militarist, Clinton as president will be used to stop this radical evolution and disguise militarism with a friendly white female face to read as a feminist achievement. "We" will be told that the glass ceiling has been broken. "We" will hear that we are now in a postfeminist era. But the particular "we" remains too rich, too white, too imperial, too capitalist, too everything that most of us are not. It is not enough to hope that this elitism will resolve itself. It is crucial for US women to say no to the policies of mass destruction, incarceration, and militarization that Hillary Clinton represents, even if an effective strategy for doing so seems unclear. Anti-imperial feminists need to resolve to say, *not in our name.*

Hillary's renewed defense of Netanyahu and Israel's "right" to defend itself asserts "rights" to a patriarchal, racist, and colonial state. She reiterates her full commitment to Netanyahu declaring herself a "life-long friend to Israel with an unbreakable bond" that she will continue into her presidency if elected.[3] Hillary endorses the same policies that have not worked for decades, embracing Israel by defending her position as one of "containment, deterrence and defeat." And this pro-Israel stance seeps into policies toward

Iran, Syria, Saudi Arabia, Turkey and other countries. She sees the ultimate responsibility for the ongoing tragedy in Gaza as Hamas's fault; she frames renewed interventionism as "smart power"—using our power "to spread freedom and democracy," but not in old forms of unilateralism and "boots on the ground." She may change tactics but not the strategy. The US remains the arbiter of goodness and righteousness. For women outside the US, this dedication to imperialism is disastrous.

Clinton speaks of balance between overreach and underreach. But in feminist opposition there is no middle ground. Her mantra is "peace, progress and prosperity." I can think of other "P's," in echo of Angela Davis: "patriarchy, prejudice, poverty, Palestine, and prisons." Feminists of every sort need to mobilize and push for a multipronged agenda, during and long after the 2016 presidential election, stand in broad coalition with others against racist, patriarchal imperialist practices wherever they exist, and demand an end to human and ecological destruction.

Clinton has long said that women's rights, and more recently, sexual violence is a key indicator of the security for any state. But sexual violence, and all forms of gender violence, increase in times of war. Hillary Clinton, as secretary of state, said she would make women's formal rights integral to foreign policy. The women in Iraq and Afghanistan are wondering what happened to that promise, and their formal or informal rights, in their war-torn countries. Think about Nigeria, Turkey, Rwanda, Syria, and Iraq. How does one seek to end sexual violence while making and condoning war, which exacerbates every sort of violence, not least rape? In February 2014, Clinton delivered a lecture at the University of Miami in which she claimed sexual violence was at the heart of violence in Syria and Libya. There is a shift in Clinton's rhetoric—from women's rights are human rights (1995) to the problem of sexual violence (2014). It's a self-serving shift, and a politically astute one, mirroring a renewed concern with sexual violence among US feminists.

US bombs were wrapped in women's rights rhetoric in the Afghan and Iraq wars. Similar problems appear in Hillary's newest drive toward yet another war, in Syria, where she continues to stake out a position far to the right of Obama, criticizing him for not being readier to go to war.

Yet these concerns with rape and with women's rights can just as easily be turned against Clinton: after all, one almost universal consequence of war is an increase in rape. And these interventions that Clinton has championed have greatly strengthened ISIS, for whom femicide and sex slavery is a way of life.

It is time to use our feminism as the basis for mobilizing for a just and real peace.

Clinton says that peace and security require the participation of women, especially in the labor force, in the formal economy. How do you "fix" the economy by simply allowing and encouraging women to enter it? And how do you "fix" women with an economy that is structured with racial and sexual ghettoes and unequal pay? This emphasis on women entering the labor force is an old strategy that intensifies the triple day of labor for women, but is not tied to their freedom, equality, or liberation. Jobs did not bring liberation to women in Russia after their revolution or to women in the US today.

Clinton uses her "No Ceilings" initiative to advance women and girls around the world. She says that "giving women the tools to fully participate in their economies, societies and governments" is the unfinished business of the twenty-first century. I am more interested in a "No Basements" initiative: feminists need to work to empower from the bottom up where most women are found—hauling water, collecting wood, standing on assembly lines or at factory sewing machines, providing food, doing low-paid service jobs.

Hillary Clinton's candidacy allows us to clarify the multiple politics of feminisms by differing with her worldview. At the time of this writing, it seems as if Hillary Clinton will become the Democratic Party's nominee for president in 2016. And it is very possible that she will win the presidency. So it is more important than ever to figure out how we can build feminist solidarities across the globe to stop Hillary's wars.

Clinton assumes the "exceptional" status of the US because of its supposed just and democratic practices, especially toward women. She long ago set her sights outside the US as in China in 1995 at the Beijing Women's Conference, where she famously declared "women's rights are human rights, and human rights are women's rights." Interestingly, despite some campaign efforts to talk about paid family leave in the United States, she has usually located the problem of women's oppression elsewhere, and not here. But what about safeguarding access to medical care, demanding a living wage and alleviations to poverty, improving day care, lessening incarceration rates, and increasing contraceptive coverage for women of color, right here in the US?

Too many Western feminists similarly view women's rights as primarily an agenda to pursue on behalf of the particularly oppressed abroad. Critiques of women's rights in Egypt, in Venezuela, in Nigeria, and so on often overlap with similar indecencies here. Data shows that the US is well behind many countries when it comes to day care policy, family leave rights, health care, and reproductive rights for women. There are women presidents now in several African and South American countries. We are hardly exceptional; in fact, we trail behind.

The "No Ceilings" report says that there "has never been a better time to be born female."[4] Really? In Syria? In Northern Nigeria? In Ferguson, Missouri? Violence against women remains at epic proportions in every single country in the world, according to Lydia Alpizar, director of the Association for Women's Rights in Development. In the US, campus rape is an epidemic at the rate of 1 in 5 women in the US, and even higher for young women who are not in college. Pregnant women are at their greatest risk in US prisons. The findings by the UN Commission on the Status of Women, now twenty years after the 1995 Declaration to bring about equality, are an outrage. The growing worldwide disparities of wealth are a feminist issue. But when it comes to torture, abortion access, equal pay, hunger, homelessness, a living wage, and so on, millions in the US also suffer, a fact that should humble us and keep our belief in American exceptionalism in check.

All the above explains why women need more than President Hillary Clinton can offer. The Black Lives Matter movement makes clear that structural and intersectional racist violence must be addressed alongside gender and sexual inequalities, across class divides, and against hetero-patriarchal white privilege. Maybe a really "exceptional" justice movement at home has already begun.

Hillary Clinton's brand of feminism—power feminism, imperial feminism, white ruling-class feminism—is not the answer to this moment of crisis. And the answer must be about so much more than gender. Anti-imperial feminism must engage the multiple and complex identities of gender—racial, class, sexual, age, ability, trans, and national.

But imperial feminism props up the structural misogyny of empire even while critiquing discrimination toward women. A woman without an inclusive anti-racist, anti-imperial feminist agenda cannot either imagine or create the conditions for peace and justice. So Clinton, by showing that a woman can lead and drive imperialism, might make a difference for a few, but she cannot make enough of a difference for most people of the suffering globe.

Instead, critique the racist, patriarchal, capitalist and global market that turns 70 percent of women into migrants and refugees. Stand against the newest expressions of structural racism and misogyny to save the planet and the rest of humanity. Begin to create the networks of solidarity and trust to end the misery that too many suffer daily. We can start, not by insulting Hillary Clinton, but by creating resistance and revolutionary alliances of refusal—refusal to go along with the cruel forms of neoliberalism she has worked so hard to enact.

Contributors

Medea Benjamin is the co-founder of the women-led peace group CODEPINK and the co-founder of the human rights group Global Exchange. She has been an advocate for social justice for more than forty years. She has been described as "one of America's most committed—and most effective—fighters for human rights" by *New York Newsday* and "one of the high profile leaders of the peace movement" by the *Los Angeles Times*. She is the author of eight books, including *Drone Warfare: Killing by Remote Control*, and her articles appear regularly in outlets such as the Huffington Post, CommonDreams, AlterNet, OtherWords, and TeleSUR.

Fred Block is a research professor of sociology at the University of California, Davis. His extended analysis of the 1996 welfare legislation, written with Margaret R. Somers, was published as "From Poverty to Perversity: Ideas, Markets, and Institutions over 200

Years of Welfare Debate" in the *American Sociological Review* (2005) and is included in their co-authored book, *The Power of Market Fundamentalism: Karl Polanyi's Critique* (Harvard University Press, 2014). His other books include *The Origins of International Economic Disorder* (1977), *Revising State Theory* (1987), and *The Vampire State* (1996).

Tressie McMillan Cottom is an assistant professor of sociology at Virginia Commonwealth University and a faculty associate at the Berkman Center for Internet & Society. She is the lead editor (with Sandy Darity of Duke University) of *Profit U: The Rise of For-Profit Higher Education* (forthcoming from AERA Books). Her second book, on inequality and for-profit higher education, is under contract with The New Press.

Cottom is also a former research fellow at the Center for Poverty Research at University of California, Davis, where she wrote a public policy brief (forthcoming) that examines the link between 1996 changes that purported to "end welfare as we know it" and the rise in for-profit workforce credentials among poor women. She is an organizing consultant for the Barnard Center for Research on Women's fortieth anniversary Scholar & Feminist conference.

Cottom is a contributing editor with *Dissent* and a contributing writer with *The Atlantic*. Her writing has also appeared in *Inside Higher Education, The Chronicle of Higher Education*, Slate, Dissent Magazine, and the *New York Times*. She has been an invited speaker at the Massachusetts Institute of Technology, the University of Virginia, Duke University, University of California, Irvine, and many other institutions.

Margaret Corvid is a professional dominatrix, columnist, and journalist based in the southwest United Kingdom. Her online writing appears most often in the *New Statesman* and the *Establishment* and periodically in the *Guardian* and on cosmopolitan.com and metro.co.uk. She is a contributing editor of *Salvage*, a quarterly journal of the revolutionary left.

Zillah Eisenstein has been writing feminist theory for the past thirty-five years. She was a professor of politics at Ithaca College for four decades and is now Distinguished Scholar in Residence there. She often writes for Al Jazeera and *The Feminist Wire*. Throughout her career her books have tracked the rise of neoliberalism both within the US and across the globe.

Her books include *The Audacity of Races and Genders: A Personal and Global Story of the 2008 Election* (London: Zed Press, 2009; New York: Palgrave, 2009), *Sexual Decoys: Gender, Race and War in Imperial Democracy* (London: Zed Press; New York: Palgrave, 2007); *Against Empire* (London: Zed Press; New York: Palgrave, 2007); *Hatreds: Racialized and Sexualized Conflicts in the 21st Century* (Routledge, 1996); *Global Obscenities: Patriarchy, Capitalism, and the Lure of Cyberfantasy* (NYU Press, 1996); and *Manmade Breast Cancers* (Cornell University Press, 2001). For more information, see http://zillaheisenstein.wordpress.com.

Liza Featherstone writes often about feminism and economic justice. She is a contributing writer to *The Nation* and the magazine's first-ever advice columnist. Also a columnist for *amNY*, Featherstone has published in many national publications including the *New York Times*, the *Washington Post*, *Ms.*, *Glamour*, *Teen Vogue*, and the *Women's Review of Books*.

She is the author of *Selling Women Short: The Landmark Battle for Workers' Rights at Wal-Mart* (Basic Books, 2005) and finishing a history of the focus group, forthcoming from OR Books. She teaches journalism at both New York University and Columbia's School of International and Public Affairs.

Belén Fernández is the author of *The Imperial Messenger: Thomas Friedman at Work* (Verso, 2011), and a political travelogue titled *Coffee With Hezbollah*, about a hitchhiking expedition in the Middle East following Israel's 2006 war on Lebanon. A 2003 graduate of Columbia University, Belén spent many years hitchhiking through various parts of the world with a friend and clocking valuable hours at an avocado packing facility in southern Spain. She is now a regular contributor to the Al Jazeera English opinion section and a contributing editor at *Jacobin* magazine. She has also written for the *London Review of Books* blog, Middle East Eye, *VICE News, The Baffler*, and many other publications. Aside from Middle Eastern and Latin American politics, her beat includes US foreign policy, militarism, capitalism, Thomas Friedman, and other things harmful to human life. Her article "Dirty White Gold" about Monsanto's contributions to the farmer suicide epidemic in India was chosen by Project Censored as one of the top censored stories and media analyses of 2012–13. Belén is a connoisseur of cheap wine and continues to eschew a fixed residence.

Amber A'Lee Frost is a writer living in Brooklyn. Her work has been featured in *Jacobin*, *The Baffler*, the *New York Observer*, and *Dangerous Minds*, as well as the collection *Rosa Luxemburg: Her Life and Legacy* (Palgrave, 2013). She serves on the editorial board of *New Politics*. Frost also teaches writing at New York University. In addition to her writing, she has been an active member of Democratic Socialists of America for seven years.

Best-selling author and broadcaster **Laura Flanders** hosts *The Laura Flanders Show* on KCET/LinkTV and TeleSUR (video and audio podcast at LauraFlanders.com). Flanders is a contributing writer to *The Nation* and *Yes!* magazines and a regular contributor to Truthout and other publications. Her books include *BUSHWOMEN: Tales of a Cynical Species* (Verso, 2004), and *Blue GRIT: True Democrats Take*

Back Politics from the Politicians (Penguin Press, 2007). Flanders was the founding host of the primetime call-in "Your Call" on public radio station KALW, and of "CounterSpin," which was produced by the media-watch group Fairness and Accuracy in Reporting. She appears regularly on MSNBC and has served as a substitute host for PBS veteran Bill Moyers. Flanders and her partner, choreographer Elizabeth Streb, co-host "Risky Talking," an annual live event with smart speakers, wild actions, and a rollicking public conversation about risk. To learn more, go to laurasflanders.com. Follow Laura on Twitter @GRITlaura.

Kathleen Geier is a writer based in Chicago. She has written about economics, feminism, labor, and politics for *The Nation*, *The Baffler*, *Washington Monthly*, *Bookforum*, and other publications. She enjoys lo-fi punk and difficult movies.

Megan Erickson is the author of *Class War: The Privatization of Childhood* (Verso, 2015). She is a New York City public school teacher and an editor at *Jacobin*.

Catherine Liu is a professor of film and media studies and visual studies at University of California, Irvine. She is the author of *American Idyll: Anti-Elitism as Cultural Critique* (University of Iowa Press, 2011) and *Copying Machines: Taking Notes for the Automaton* (University of Minnesota Press, 2000). She is also the author of the 2012 novel *Oriental Girls Desire Romance*. She has recently completed a memoir of middle-aged emancipation titled *Panda Gifts*.

Donna Murch is an associate professor of history at Rutgers University. She is currently completing a trade press book, *Crack in Los Angeles: Policing the Crisis and the War on Drugs*, which explores the militarization of law enforcement, the social history of drug consumption and sale, and the political economy of mass incarceration in late twentieth-century California. In 2010, Murch published *Living for the City: Migration, Education and the Rise of the Black Panther Party in Oakland, California* with the University of North Carolina Press, which won the Phillis Wheatley Prize in December 2011. She has written for the *Black Scholar, Souls, Journal of Urban History, Journal of American History, OAH Magazine of History, Perspectives, New Politics, Jacobin,* and *Boston Review.* Murch also co-edited a special edition of the *Journal of Urban History* on mass incarceration and urban spaces for the September 2015 issue.

Yasmin Nair is a writer, academic, and activist in Chicago. She's a co-founder of the radical queer editorial collective Against Equality and the volunteer policy director of Gender JUST. Her work has appeared in several publications and anthologies including the Electronic Intifada, *In These Times,* The Daily Dot, and *Maximumrocknroll.* She is currently working on a book titled *Strange Love: Neoliberalism, Affect and the Invention of Social Justice.* Nair's writings can be found at yasminnair.net.

Frances Fox Piven is one of the most important social scientists of the last century. Her groundbreaking work with Richard A. Cloward on the functions of social welfare and poor relief (*Regulating the Poor,* 1971) ignited a scholarly debate that reshaped the field of social welfare policy. Subsequent work analyzed the conditions under which the disruptive actions of the poor influenced the foundation of the modern American welfare state (*Poor People's Movements,* 1977) and were necessary to the advancement of progressive social policy and political reforms (*The Breaking of the American Social Compact,* 1997; *Challenging Authority,* 2008). Piven and Cloward also authored *Why Americans Don't Vote* in 1988 and *Why Americans Still Don't Vote and Why Politicians Want It That Way* in 2000. Piven is the author or co-author of more than 200 articles published in academic journals, books, popular publications, and journals of opinion.

A co-founder of the National Welfare Rights Organization, Piven also co-founded the Human Service Employees Registration and Voter Education Campaign, which pioneered the idea of "automatic voter registration," whereby citizens would be registered to vote when they applied for social assistance or drivers' licenses. She teaches at the CUNY Graduate Center.

Maureen Tkacik is a full-time mom and part-time waitress in Washington, DC. She is a founding editor of Jezebel and a former *Wall Street Journal* reporter. An essayist and a financial journalist, her work appears in *Columbia Journalism Review, The Baffler, The Nation,* and many other publications.

Notes

Prologue

1. Chris Isidore, "Bailout Plan Rejected—Supporters Scramble," CNN-Money, September 29, 2008.
2. Cora Currier, "The Kill Chain: The Lethal Bureaucracy Behind Obama's Drone War," The Intercept, October 15, 2015.
3. James Cavallaro, Stephan Sonnenberg, and Sarah Knuckey, *Living Under Drones: Death, Injury and Trauma to Civilians from US Drone Practices in Pakistan*, Stanford, CA: International Human Rights and Conflict Resolution Clinic, Stanford Law School; New York: NYU School of Law, Global Justice Clinic, 2012.
4. Thom Shanker, "U.S. Foreign Arms Sales Are Most of Global Market," *New York Times*, August 27, 2012.
5. "Terrorism Finance: Action Request for Senior-Level Engagement on Terrorism Finance", December 30, 2009, WikiLeaks.
6. "Editorial: Why Won't the US Sign a Land Mine Treaty?" *National Catholic Reporter*, July 16, 2014.
7. Hillary Clinton, *Hard Choices*, New York: Simon & Schuster, 2014, 359.
8. Greg Shupak, "Libya and Its Contexts," *Jacobin*, September 2, 2013.

9. Eliott C. McLaughlin, "ISIS Executes More Christians in Libya, Video Shows," cnn.com, April 20, 2015.

Introduction

1. Katha Pollitt, "Why I'm Ready—and Excited—for Hillary," *The Nation*, June 2, 2015.
2. Gloria Steinem, "Why the White House Needs Hillary Clinton," *The Guardian*, October 19, 2015.
3. Francine Prose, "New York Supergals Love That Naughty Prez," *New York Observer*, September 2, 1998.
4. "Who's Ready for Hillary?" *The Nation*, November 24, 2014.
5. BlankBeat, "Hillary Can't Even Win a Debate Without Being Told She Sucks by the Internet," DailyKos, October 15, 2015.
6. Amanda Marcotte, "Just Admit Hillary Won! The Silly Sexism of the Fox News/Lefty Smartypants Crowd," Salon, October 14, 2015.
7. Amanda Reed, "Walmart and Sex Discrimination," Now.org/ blog, June 6, 2013.
8. "Video: Hillary Clinton in 1990: I'm 'Proud of Wal-Mart'," truthdig. com, May 25, 2015.
9. Christopher Massie, "Hillary Clinton Used to Talk About How the People on Welfare Were 'No Longer Deadbeats'," BuzzFeed News, July 21, 2015.
10. Rachel Cromidas, "Gloria Steinem and Roxane Gay: It's Time for a Female President," chicagoist.com, October 30, 2015.
11. Amanda Marcotte, "Let's Storm the Sanders' He-Man Women-Haters Club: Hillary Plays the Gender Card, While Bernie Fans Rage," Salon, October 26, 2015.

1. Hillary Clinton, Economic Populist

1. Emma Roller, "How Hillary Clinton Once Disappointed Elizabeth Warren on Wall Street Reform," nationaljournal.com, September 5, 2014.
2. Elizabeth Warren and Amelia Warren Tyagi, *The Two Income Trap: Why Middle-Class Parents Are Going Broke*, New York: Basic Books, 2003, 126.
3. Gwen Ifill, "The 1992 Campaign; Hillary Clinton Defends Her Conduct in Law Firm," *New York Times*, March 17, 1992.
4. "Hillary D. Rodham's 1969 Student Commencement Speech," wellesley. edu.

5. Carl Bernstein, *A Woman in Charge: The Life of Hillary Rodham Clinton*, New York: Vintage, 2007, 70.

6. Susan B. Garland and Dean Foust, "Hillary Clinton, Go Go Getter," *Bloomberg Business*, April 17, 1994.

7. Brian Ross, Maddy Sauer, and Rhonda Schwartz, "Clinton Remained Silent as Wal-Mart Fought Unions," abcnews.go.com, January 31, 2008.

8. Hillary Rodham Clinton, *Living History*, New York: Simon & Schuster, 2003, 111.

9. Robert E. Scott, "NAFTA's Legacy: Growing U.S. Trade Deficits Cost 682,900 Jobs," Economic Policy Institute, December 17, 2013.

10. Derek Willis, "The Senate Votes that Divided Hillary Clinton and Bernie Sanders," *New York Times*, May 27, 2015.

11. Brody Mullins, Peter Nicholas, and Rebecca Ballhaus, "The Bill and Hillary Clinton Money Machine Taps Corporate Cash," *Wall Street Journal*, July 1, 2014.

12. James V. Grimaldi and Rebecca Ballhaus, "Hillary Clinton's Complex Corporate Ties," *Wall Street Journal*, February 19, 2015.

13. David Sirota, Andrew Perez, and Matthew Cunningham-Cook, "As Colombian Oil Money Flowed to Clintons, State Department Took No Action to Prevent Labor Violations," IBT, April 8, 2015. See also "Clintons Stand Up for Colombia" (editorial) *Investor's Business Daily*, June 11, 2010.

14. Rick Cohen, "Clinton Foundation Charged with Providing Shoddy and Dangerous Emergency Shelters in Haiti," NPQ, July 20, 2011.

15. Brad DeLong, "Hoisted from the Archives: Review of Johnson and Broder, The System," delong.typepad.com, October 29, 2007.

16. Josh Bivens and Lawrence Mishel, "The Pay of Corporate Executives and Financial Executives as Evidence of Rents in Top 1 Percent Incomes," *Journal of Economic Perspectives* 27: 3, 2013, 57–78; "Did Financialization Reduce Economic Growth?" *Socio-Economic Review*, 2015, ser.oxford journals.org.

17. Eric Dash and Julie Creswell, "Citigroup Saw No Red Flags Even as It Made Bolder Bets," *New York Times*, November 22, 2009.

18. William D. Cohan, "Rethinking Robert Rubin," *Bloomberg Business*, September 30, 2012.

19. Robert E. Rubin and Jacob Weisberg, *In an Uncertain World: Tough Choices From Wall Street to Washington*, New York: Random House, 2004, 128.

20. Ibid., 153.

21. William D. Cohan, "A First Person History Lesson From Robert Rubin,"

New York Times, November 19, 2014; Kevin G. Hall, "Clinton's Economic Advisors Served Her Husband," McClatchyDC, April 7, 2008.

22. William D. Cohan, "Why Wall Street Loves Hillary," Politico, November 11, 2014.

23. Gail Sheehy, "Hillaryland at War," *Vanity Fair*, July 31, 2008; Jeanne Cummings, "Hillary Clinton the Populist?" Politico, March 24, 2008.

24. "Hillary Clinton Transcript: Building the 'Growth and Fairness Economy'," blogs.wsj.com, July 13, 2015.

25. James Kwak, "Hillary Clinton's Weak Plans for Changing Wall Street," *The Atlantic*, October 9, 2015.

26. Ben White, "Clinton Speech React: Is That It?" Politico, July 13, 2015.

27. Cohan, "Why Wall Street Loves Hillary"; Louis Jacobson, "Meme Says Hillary Clinton's Top Donors Are Banks and Corporations, Bernie Sanders' Are Labor Unions," PolitiFact, July 7, 2015.

28. Mullins et al., "The Bill and Hillary Clinton Money Machine".

29. Ashley C. Allen, "Report: The 10 Richest U.S. Presidents," *USA Today*, February 17, 2015.

30. Lisa Lerer and Lauren Streib, "Clinton Earns $12 Million Speaking, Writing After Service," Bloomberg Business, July 21, 2014.

31. Maggie Haberman and Steve Eder, "Clintons Earned $30 Million in 16 Months, Report Shows," *New York Times*, May 15, 2015; Matea Gold, Rosalind S. Helderman, and Anne Gearan, "Clintons Have Made More Than $25 Million for Speaking since January 2014," *Washington Post*, May 15, 2015.

32. Anne Bruzgulis, "Liberal Group Claims All of Hillary Clinton's Speaking Fees Went to Charity," Punditfact, June 16, 2015.

33. Carmen DeNavas Walt and Bernadette D. Proctor, "Income and Poverty in the United States: 2014," census.gov, September 2015.

34. Laura Myers, "High Fashion, Expense for Hillary Travel," *Las Vegas Review-Journal*, August 16, 2014.

35. Jon Greenberg, "Hillary Clinton Says She and Bill Were 'Dead Broke'," PolitiFact, June 10, 2014.

36. Matthew Goldstein and Steve Eder, "For Clintons, a Hedge Fund in the Family," *New York Times*, March 22, 2015.

37. Larry M. Bartels, "The Social Welfare Deficit: Public Opinion, Policy Responsiveness, and Political Inequality in Affluent Democracies," piketty.pse.ens.fr/files/Bartels2015.pdf.

38. Martin Gilens and Benjamin Page, "Testing Theories of American Politics: Elites, Interest Groups, and Average Citizens," *Perspectives on Politics* 12: 3, 2014, 575.

39. Nicholas Confessore, Sarah Cohen, and Karen Yourish, "Small Pool of Rich Donors Dominates Election Giving," *New York Times*, August 1, 2015.

2. Ending Poverty as We Know It

1. There is much controversy over the proper way to measure poverty. The method used by the US government draws on an "absolute" measure that estimates what people need to subsist at a minimal level. International data measures "relative" poverty calculated as those living at less than half of the median income for all households. Christopher Jencks ("The War on Poverty: Was It Lost," *New York Review of Books*, April 2, 2015) makes an optimistic case by taking "in kind" benefits into account. For a more sober analysis that draws on measures of relative poverty, see the studies in Timothy M. Smeeding, Robert Erikson, and Markus Jantti, eds., *Persistence, Privilege, and Parenting: The Comparative Study of Intergenerational Mobility*, New York: Russell Sage, 2011.
2. See Kathryn J. Edin and H. Luke Shaefer, *$2.00 a Day: Living on Almost Nothing in America*, Boston: Houghton Mifflin, 2015.
3. Melissa Hennenberger, "Will Hillary Clinton Run Against Her Husband's Welfare Legacy?" Bloomberg Business, May 26, 2015.
4. One exception was Barbara Ehrenreich, "The New Right Attack on Social Welfare," in Fred Block, Richard A. Cloward, Barbara Ehrenreich, and Frances Fox Piven, eds., *The Mean Season*, New York: Pantheon, 1987, 161–95.
5. TANF limits cumulative lifetime benefits to sixty months and requires that recipients be employed after accumulating twenty-four months. For a discussion of these limits in light of the dynamics of welfare uptake, see Greg Duncan and Gretchen Caspary, "Welfare Dynamics and the 1996 Welfare Reform," *Notre Dame Journal of Law, Ethics & Public Policy* 11: 2, 1997, 605–32.
6. Ladonna Pavetti, Ife Finch, and Liz Schott, "TANF Emerging from the Downturn a Weaker Safety Net," Center for Budget and Policy Priorities, March 1, 2013.
7. See Mark Dudzic and Adolph Reed, Jr., "The Crisis of Labour and the Left in the United States," *Socialist Register* 51, 2015.
8. Sweden has recently begun a series of small experiments with shorter hours. See David Crouch, "Efficiency Up, Turnover Down: Sweden Experiments With Six-Hour Working Day," *The Guardian*, September 17, 2015.

9. On Reich and Stiglitz, see the Basic Income Earth Network at basicincome.org/?s=Reich. Atkinson proposes a "participation income" that would be contingent on care or study or volunteer work. Anthony Atkinson, *Inequality: What Can Be Done?* Cambridge: Harvard University Press, 2015.

10. The programs are sometimes known by the name "conditional cash transfers." Compared to Western cash assistance programs, however, the conditions are benign, involving as they do the requirement that parents send their children to school and take them to see a doctor. See J. Johannsen, L. Tejerina, and A. Glassman, "Conditional Cash Transfers in Latin America: Problems and Opportunities," Inter-American Development Bank Working Paper, 2009, publications.iadb.org/handle/11319/2530?locale-attribute=en. For a discussion, see Frances Fox Piven and Lorraine Minnite, "Crisis, Convulsion and the Welfare State," in Kevin Farnsworth and Zoë Irving, eds., *Social Policy in Times of Austerity: Global Economic Crisis and the New Politics of Welfare* (Bristol, UK: Policy Press, 2015).

11. International Labour Organization, *World Social Protection Report 2014/15: Building Economic Recovery, Inclusive Development and Social Justice,* Geneva: Author, 2014; International Labour Organization, *World Social Security Report,* 2nd ed., Geneva: Author, 2014, socialprotection floor.org

12. United Nations, Economic Commission for Latin America and the Caribbean, "Social Panorama of Latin America 2012," briefing paper, cepal.org/publicaciones/xml/4/48454/SocialPanorama2012DocI.pdf. See also Erdem Yörük, "Welfare Provision as Political Containment: The Politics of Social Assistance and the Kurdish Conflict in Turkey," *Politics and Society* 40: 4, 517–47.

13. Eduardo Porter reports that Abhjit Banerjee and his colleagues at the Massachusetts Institute of Technology assessed the effects of seven cash transfer programs in Mexico, Morocco, Honduras, Nicaragua, and the Philippines and found no evidence that the programs discourage work. See Eduardo Porter, "The Myth of Welfare's Corrupting Influence on the Poor," *New York Times,* October 20, 2015.

3. Free the Children!

1. Shulamith Firestone, *The Dialectic of Sex: The Case for Feminist Revolution,* New York: William Morrow, 1970, 72.

2. Ibid., 91.

3. The article was published in *Harvard Educational Review* 43: 4, 1973, 487–514.

4. The essay was published in Patricia A. Vardin and Ilene N. Brooks, eds., *Children's Rights: Contemporary Perspectives,* New York: Teachers College Press, 1979.

5. David Brock, *The Seduction of Hillary Rodham Clinton,* New York: Free Press, 1996, 270.

6. Ibid., 120.

7. Hillary Rodham Clinton, "In France, Day Care Is Every Child's Right," *New York Times,* April 7, 1990.

8. Rebecca Traister, "Meet the New, Old Hillary," *The New Republic,* June 14, 2015.

9. Ibid.

10. Press release, "Children's Defense Fund Honors Hillary Rodham Clinton at 40th Anniversary Celebration," childrensdefense.org, September 30, 2013.

11. Daniel Denvir, "The Betrayal That Should Haunt Hillary Clinton: How She Sold Out Working Women & Never Apologized," Salon, November 2, 2015.

4. Waging War on Teachers

1. Michael Kelly, "The Inauguration; The First Couple: A Union of Mind and Ambition," *New York Times,* January 20, 1993.

2. Campaigning for Hillary at a Bronx County Democratic Rally in New York City in 2000, Bill Clinton remarked, "I'll tell you something about Hillary. She knows more—she know more about children and family, about education and health care, about how to bring economic opportunity to distressed areas than anybody I can imagine who could be running for President. She has worked on this stuff, some of these issues for 20 years, some of these issues for 30 years … She has met every test. She has worked her heart out for 16 months. She has come to every community; she's been there for you." Bill Clinton, *Public Papers of the Presidents of the United States, William J. Clinton,* Washington, DC: Office of the Federal Register, National Archives and Records Administration, 1994, 2462.

3. Carl Bernstein, *A Woman in Charge: The Life of Hillary Rodham Clinton,* New York: Vintage, 2007, Kindle loc. 3513.

4. John D. Gartner, *In Search of Bill Clinton: A Psychological Biography,* New York: St. Martin's Press, 2008, 171.

5. William H. Chafe, *Bill and Hillary: The Politics of the Personal*, New York: Farrar, Straus and Giroux, 2012, 117.
6. Bernstein, *A Woman in Charge*, Kindle loc. 3588.
7. Ibid., Kindle loc. 3562.
8. Brock, *The Seduction of Hillary Rodham Clinton*, 161.
9. Maureen Sullivan, "Hillary Clinton on Education: 8 Things the Presidential Candidate Wants You to Know," *Forbes*, April 1, 2015.
10. Bernstein, *A Woman in Charge*, Kindle loc. 1338 .
11. Chafe, *Bill and Hillary*, 119.
12. Christopher T. Cross, *Political Education: National Policy Comes of Age*, New York: Teachers College Press, 2004, 97.
13. Ibid., 94–5.
14. Linda Darling-Hammond, *The Flat World and Education: How America's Commitment to Equity Will Determine Our Future*, New York: Teachers College Press, 2010; Julian Vasquez Heilig, "Top Ten List: Why 'Choice' Demonstrates That Money Matters," National Education Policy Center, April 18, 2013; David C. Berliner, *50 Myths & Lies That Threaten America's Public Schools: The Real Crisis in Education*, New York: Teachers College Press, 2014.
15. Richard Rothstein, "Fact-Challenged Policy," Economic Policy Institute, March 11, 2011; Berliner, *50 Myths & Lies That Threaten America's Public Schools*.
16. Julie Miller, "In New Role, Hillary Clinton Treading on Familiar Policy Turf," *Education Week*, April 14, 1993.

5. Neoliberal Fictions

1. Adam Gopnik, "Harper Lee's Failed Novel About Race," *New Yorker*, July 27, 2015.
2. See Michiko Kakutani's *New York Times* essay ("Review: Harper Lee's 'Go Set a Watchman' Gives Atticus Finch a Dark Side," July 11, 2015), in which she expressed concerns for the book's fans; and Melissa Locker, "To Kill a Mockingbird Fans May Not Like the New Atticus Finch," *Vanity Fair*, July 11, 2015. Randall Kennedy argues ("Harper Lee's 'Go Set a Watchman'," *New York Times Sunday Book Review*, July 14, 2015) that *Watchman* offers a less sentimental and more accurate appraisal of Atticus.
3. In the op-ed pages of the *New York Times* (July 25, 2015), Joe Nocera calls the publication of *Go Set a Watchman* a "fraud."
4. Eileen Reynolds, "To Kill a Mockingbird at 50," *New Yorker*, June 14, 2010.

5. Joe Nocera, "Harper Lee's 'Go Set a Watchman' Fraud," *New York Times*, July 25, 2015.

6. In *The Cultural Cold War* (New York: New Press, 2013), Frances Stonor Saunders argues that American cultural hegemony took place through the coordinated efforts of government-funded foundations with a "private" front and the Ford and Rockefeller Foundations to promote American culture abroad.

7. Adolph Reed, "The Limits of Anti-Racism," *Left Business Observer* 121, September 2009.

8. Michael Young, *The Rise of the Meritocracy*, New York, London: Transaction, 1994. Christopher Hayes emphasizes the "left's" belief in the meritocracy as a mechanism for realizing economic and social justice in *Twilight of the Elites: America After Meritocracy*, New York: Broadway Paperbacks, 2012.

9. Kevin Cirilli, "Bill Clinton Defends Repeal of Glass Steagall," The Hill, August 11, 2015.

10. Lily Geismer, *Don't Blame Us: Suburban Liberals and the Transformation of the Democratic Party*, Princeton: Princeton University Press, 2014.

11. Jennifer Silva, *Coming Up Short: Working Class Adulthood in an Age of Uncertainty*, New York and London: Oxford University Press, 2013.

12. Doug Henwood, "Stop Hillary! Vote No to a Clinton Dynasty," *Harper's Magazine*, November 2014.

13. The Personal Responsibility and Work Reconciliation Act of 1996 included a variety of penalties on states and individuals who were unable to abide by the stringent requirements of the federal block grants allocated to help the poor transition to work. States had to keep their welfare rolls at 75 percent of the 1994 budgets. States that could not demonstrate that steady increase in employment targets would see their block grants slashed. Lifetime benefits were restricted to five years. Legal immigrants were no longer eligible for welfare.

14. Seth Ackerman, "Yes, Racism Is Rooted in Economic Inequality: Some Notes on a Recent Controversy," *Jacobin*, July 29, 2015.

6. The Great Ambivalence

1. Richard Rubin and Jennifer Epstein, "Hillary and Bill Clinton Made $139 Million in Eight Years, Bloomberg Business, July 31, 2015.

2. Press release, "Ernesto Zedillo Becomes Presidential Counselor at Laureate International Universities," April 24, 2015, laureate.net.

3. Sara Goldrick-Rab, and Andrew Kelly, eds., *Reinventing Financial Aid:*

Charting a New Course to College Affordability, Cambridge, MA: Harvard Education Press, 2014.

4. Ben Smith, "Clinton and Obama, Johnson and King," *Politico*, January 7, 2008.

7. The Clintons' War on Drugs

1. Michelle Alexander, *The New Jim Crow: Mass Incarceration in the Age of Colorblindness*, New York: The New Press, 2010; Naomi Murakawa, *The First Civil Right: How Liberals Built Prison America*, New York: Oxford University Press, 2014; Christian Parenti, *Lockdown America: Police and Prisons in the Age of Crisis*, New York: Verso, 1999.

2. "Full Video of Hillary Clinton's Meeting with Black Lives Matters Activists," *Democracy Now!*, August 19, 2015.

3. See my review of recent scholarship about the Rockefeller era for context. Donna Murch, "Who's to Blame for Mass Incarceration?" *Boston Review*, October 16, 2015.

4. "Full Video of Hillary Clinton's Meeting."

5. Lee Fang, "Private Prison Lobbyists Are Raising Cash for Hillary Clinton," *The Intercept*, July 23, 2015.

6. Alexander, *The New Jim Crow*, 9.

7. While incarceration rates are much worse for black men, rates for black women in the United States are also high: as of 2001, lifetime rates were 1 in 19 for black women compared to 1 in 181 for white women. The Sentencing Project, "Incarcerated Women Fact Sheet" (revised September 2012).

8. Alexander, *The New Jim Crow*.

9. Jon F. Hale, "The Making of the New Democrats," *Political Science Quarterly* 110: 2, 1995, 215.

10. Ibid., 212.

11. Ibid., 218–25; Thomas Ferguson and Joel Rogers, *Right Turn: The Decline of the Democrats and the Future of American Politics*, New York: Hill and Wang, 1986.

12. Robert C. Smith, *We Have No Leaders: African Americans in the Post-Civil Rights Era*, Albany: State University of New York Press, 1996, 256.

13. This whole section is heavily indebted to the pathbreaking research of eminent political scientist Robert C. Smith; see Smith, *We Have No Leaders*, 255–7. I was not able to obtain a copy of the report, but I am including its full citation for those interested in further research. Milton Kotler and Nelson Rosenbaum, "Strengthening the Democratic Party

through Strategic Marketing: Voters and Donors," a confidential report for the Democratic National Committee by the CRG Research Institute, Washington, DC, 1985. Stanley Greenberg, *Report on Democratic Defection*, Washington, DC, 1985, as quoted in Thomas Edsall and Mary Edsall, *Chain Reaction: The Impact of Race, Rights and Taxes on American Politics*, New York: W.W. Norton, 1992, 182. The Edsalls published an article succinctly titled "Race" in the *Atlantic Monthly* in 1991 that parroted similar claims.

14. Smith, *We Have No Leaders*, 255.

15. Ferguson and Rogers, *Right Turn*, 207–32; Lance Selfa, *The Democrats: A Critical History*, Chicago: Haymarket, 2008, 63–85; Ian Haney López, *Dog Whistle Politics: How Coded Racial Appeals Have Reinvented Racism and Wrecked the Middle Class*, New York: Oxford University Press, 2014.

16. Hale, "The Making of the New Democrats," 225.

17. "Willie Horton 1988 Attack Ad," available on YouTube.

18. Jonathan Simon, *Governing Through Crime: How the War on Crime Transformed American Democracy and Created a Culture of Fear*, New York: Oxford University Press, 2007, 57.

19. Hale, "The Making of the New Democrats," 221–5.

20. Ibid., 226–7. For collusion of the Congressional Black Caucus in the Reagan-era drug war, see Donna Murch, "Crack in Los Angeles: Crisis, Militarization and African American Response to the Late Twentieth Century War on Drugs," *Journal of American History* 102: 1, Summer 2015, 162–73.

21. Marshall Frady, "Death in Arkansas," *New Yorker*, February 22, 1993, 107, 126–32; Simon, *Governing Through Crime*, 69.

22. Simon, *Governing Through Crime*, 66–70; Frady, "Death in Arkansas," 132.

23. Paul D'Amato, "The Democrats and the Death Penalty," *International Socialist Review* 6, Spring 1999.

24. Selfa, *The Democrats*, 79.

25. This quotation is taken from a summary by Naomi Murakawa, *The First Civil Right*, 143.

26. Alexander, *The New Jim Crow*, 55.

27. Gerald Horne, "Black Fire: 'Riot' and 'Revolt' in Los Angeles, 1965 and 1992," Lawrence B. DeGraaf, Kevin Mulroy, and Quintard Taylor, eds., *Seeking El Dorado: African Americans in California*, Seattle: University of Washington Press, 2015, 377–404; Murakawa, *The First Civil Right*, 142; Parenti, *Lockdown America*, 63–6.

28. Fang, "Private Prison Lobbyists Are Raising Cash"; Helen Redmond,

"Are the Drug Warriors Ready to Surrender?" *Socialist Worker*, August 26, 2015.

29. Dan Merica, "Bill Clinton Says He Made Mass Incarceration Issue Worse," cnn.com, July 15, 2015.

30. Alexander, *The New Jim Crow*, 55.

31. Ibid., 58–94; D'Amato, "The Democrats and the Death Penalty."

32. Selfa, *The Democrats*, 79.

33. Murakawa, *The First Civil Right*, 141–6.

34. Selfa, *The Democrats*, 84.

35. Robert Parry, "Ronald Reagan: Worst President Ever?" Common Dreams, June 3, 2009.

36. Charles P. Pierce, "Bill Clinton Apologizes for His Role in America's Prison Epidemic," *Esquire*, July 16, 2015.

37. Several scholars have explored how the incarcerated, convicted felons, and illicit drug users and sellers have come to signify the antithesis of citizenship. See, for example, Julilly Kohler Hausmann, "'The Attila the Hun Law': New York's Rockefeller Drug Laws and the Making of a Punitive State," *Journal of Social History* 44: 1, 2010, 71–95.

38. Patrick Healy and Katharine Q. Seelye, "Clinton Says She 'Mispoke' About Dodging Sniper Fire," *New York Times*, March 25, 2008; Robert Parry, "Hillary Clinton's Failed Libya Doctrine," Consortiumnews.com, October 22, 2015.

8. Marry the State, Jail the People

1. Sanders pledged to abolish the private prison system, following repeated criticisms from the group Black Lives Matter and other activists that he paid insufficient attention to the issue of mass incarceration in the United States. Carimah Townes, "Bernie Sanders Unveils Ambitious Plan to End Private Prisons," *Think Progress*, September 17, 2015.

2. Fang, "Private Prison Lobbyists Are Raising Cash."

3. Rebecca Burns, "VAWA: A Victory for Women, but Which Women?" *In These Times*, February 28, 2013.

4. "Incarcerated Women," The Sentencing Project, September 2012.

5. Emily Bazelon, "Purvi Patel Could Be Just the Beginning," *New York Times*, April 1, 2015.

6. Alex Campbell, "Battered Woman Faces 15 More Years in Prison after Losing Clemency Plea," BuzzFeed News, September 23, 2015.

7. Elizabeth Bernstein, "Militarized Humanitarianism Meets Carceral Feminism: The Politics of Sex, Rights, and Freedom in Contemporary

Antitrafficking Campaigns," Interdisciplinary Project on Human Trafficking, traffickingroundtable.org, January 2, 2011; Janet Halley, Prabha Kotiswaran, Hila Shamir, and Chantal Thomas, "From the International to the Local in Feminist Legal Responses to Rape, Prostitution/Sex Work, and Sex Trafficking: Four Studies in Contemporary Governance Feminism," *Harvard Journal of Law and Gender* 29, 2006, 335–423.

8. Doug Henwood, "Stop Hillary! Vote No to a Clinton Dynasty," *Harper's Magazine,* November 2014; Henwood, *My Turn: Hillary Clinton Targets the Presidency,* New York: O/R Books, 2016.

9. Laura Carlsen, "What We've Learned from NAFTA," *New York Times,* November 23, 2015.

10. Rebecca Bohrman and Naomi Murakawa, "Remaking Big Government: Immigration and Crime Control in the United States," in Julia Sudbury and Asale Angel-Ajani, eds., *Global Lockdown: Women of Color and the Global Prison Industrial Complex,* New York: Routledge, 2005, 109–26.

11. Monica Potts, "A Second Chance for Low-Income Men," New America Foundation, April 2, 2014.

12. Burns, "VAWA."

13. "Statement on British 'Aid Cut' Threats to African Countries that Violate LBGTI rights," Pambazuka News, pambazuka.net/en/category.php/advocacy/77470, October 27, 2011.

14. Karma Chavez, "Pushing Boundaries: Queer Intercultural Communication," *Journal of International and Intercultural Communication,* 6:2, May 2013, 83.

9. Abortion and the Politics of Failure

1. Esmé E. Deprez, "The Vanishing U.S. Abortion Clinic," BloombergView, December 8, 2015.

2. Erica Hellerstein, "The Rise of the DIY Abortion in Texas," *The Atlantic,* June 27, 2014; Laura Tillman, "Desperate U.S. Women Forced to Go to Mexico to Take Care of Unwanted Pregnancies," AlterNet, August 29, 2010.

3. Texas Policy Evaluation Project, "Research Brief: Texas Women's Experiences Attempting Self-Induced Abortion in the Face of Dwindling Options," https://utexas.app.box.com/WExSelfInductionResearchBrief, November 17, 2015.

4. James Brooke, "Ulcer Drug Tied to Numerous Abortions in Brazil," *New York Times,* May 19, 1993.

5. Martha Dubose, "The Search for an Ideal Contraceptive," *Sydney Morning Herald*, November 10, 1971.
6. Gina Kolata, "Business Dispute May Delay Introduction of Abortion Pill," *New York Times*, November 1, 1996.
7. "Around the Globe," *Life Communications* 4: 19, November 1994, iclnet. org; Zina Mouhkeiber, "Faith Healers," *Forbes*, October 28, 2002.

10. Hillary Screws Sex Workers

1. "Conversation With Sen. Clinton," archive.rgj.com, April 29, 2007.
2. Laura Agustín, *Sex at the Margins: Migration, Labour Markets and the Rescue Industry*, London: Zed Books, 1988, 36–7.
3. "Hillary Clinton on Human Trafficking," Address to Organization for Security and Co-operation in Europe, September 14–15, 2009, available on YouTube.
4. Robin D., "Big Mother Is Watching You: Hillary Clinton," Tits and Sass, April 14, 2015.
5. Abigail Pesta, "Somaly Mum's Story: 'I didn't lie,'" *Marie Claire*, September 16, 2014.
6. William Shaw and Kuch Naren," AFESIP Blames Official in Response to Charges," *Cambodia Daily*, January 13, 2005.
6. Taylor Wofford, "Somaly Mam Foundation Closes," *Newsweek*, October 20, 2014.
7. Lawrence Gostin, "JAMA Forum: The Anti-Prostitution 'Loyalty Oath'," news@JAMA, February 13, 2013.
8. Anne Elizabeth Moore, "Special Report: Money and Lies in Anti-Human Trafficking NGOs," Truthout, January 27, 2015.
9. Ignatio Torres, "Why Sex Workers of Nevada's Moonlite Bunny Ranch Are Ready for Hillary Clinton in 2016," fusion.net, May 12, 2015.
10. Bella Robinson, "The Effects of Polaris Project in Rhode Island," docs. google.com.
11. Tara Burns, "How to Decriminalize Prostitution in the United States," taraburns.net, September 3, 2015.

11. Hillary Does Honduras

1. Jim Lobe, "Honduras: Obama Declares Coup 'Not Legal' Amid Uncertainty," Inter Press Service News Agency, June 29, 2009.
2. Belén Fernández, "US Ambassador Hugo Llorens Discloses Secrets of

the Honduran Coup; Chinese Viewing Prohibited," The Narco News Bulletin, August 15, 2009.

3. Hillary Rodham Clinton, *Hard Choices*, New York: Simon & Schuster, 2014, 222.

4. Ibid., 266.

5. Lee Fang, "During Honduras Crisis, Clinton Suggested Back Channel With Lobbyist Lanny Davis," The Intercept, July 6, 2015.

6. Lanny J. Davis, "The Way Forward in Honduras," *Wall Street Journal*, November 9, 2009.

7. Dana Frank, "In Honduras, a Mess Made in the U.S.," *New York Times*, January 26, 2012.

8. John O'Callaghan, "Obama Hails Return of Honduras to Democratic Fold," Reuters, October 5, 2011.

9. "Dolares falsos financiarian protestas en Honduras," *El Heraldo*, March 28, 2011.

10. Adrian Pine "Jeremy Spector (State Dept) blames victims of Lobo's repression for Lobo's repression," Quotha, March 31, 2011.

11. Mark Weisbrot, "Hard Choices: Hillary Clinton Admits Role in Honduran Coup Aftermath," Al Jazeera America, September 29, 2014.

12. Jeffrey Goldberg, "Hillary Clinton: 'Failure' to Help Syrian Rebels Led to the Rise of ISIS," *The Atlantic*, August 10, 2014.

13. Kevin Young and Diana C. Sierra Becerra, "Hillary Clinton's Empowerment," *Jacobin*, September 3, 2015.

14. Frank, "In Honduras, a Mess made by the U.S."

15. Weisbrot, "Hard Choices."

12. *Pink-Slipping Hillary*

1. Harold Hongju Koh, "The Obama Administration and International Law," US Department of State, March 25, 2010.

2. Paul Steinhauser and John Helton, "CNN Poll: Public Against Syria Strike Resolution," cnn.com, September 9, 2013.

3. Ken Thomas, "Clinton Would Push for No-Fly Zone," *US News and World Report*, October 2, 2015.

4. "Press Release: Sanders Statement on Syria," berniesanders.com 2016, October 3, 2015.

5. David Morgan, "Clinton Says U.S. Could 'Totally Obliterate' Iran," Reuters, April 22, 2008.

6. Avner Cohen and William Burr, eds., "The U.S. Discovery of Israel's Secret Nuclear Project," National Security Archive, April 15, 2015.

7. Jessica Schulberg, "Hillary Clinton Promises a More Muscular Foreign Policy as President," Huffington Post, September 9, 2015.
8. Glenn Greenwald, "Hillary Clinton Goes to Militaristic, Hawkish Think Tank, Gives Militaristic, Hawkish Speech," The Intercept, September 9, 2015.
9. Ben Jacobs, "Hillary Clinton Condemns Anti-Israel Boycotts as 'Counterproductive'," The Guardian, July 7, 2015.
10. Nick Gass, "Clinton: Putin's Ability to Grab Presidency Has a Certain Appeal," Politico, September 9, 2015.
11. Jason Horowitz, "Events in Iraq Open Door for Interventionist Revival, Historian Says," New York Times, June 15, 2014.

13. Beyond Hillary

1. Rania Baker, "Palestinians Express 'Solidarity With the People of Ferguson,' in Mike Brown Statement," Electronic Intifada, August 15, 2014.
2. Rania Khalek, "Israel Trained Police 'Occupy' Missouri After Killing of Black Youth," Dispatches from the Underclass, August 15, 2014.
3. Hillary Clinton, "How I Would Reaffirm Unbreakable Bond With Israel and Benjamin Netanyahu," The Forward, November 4, 2015.
4. "No Ceilings: The Full Participation Report," published March 2015 by the Clinton Foundation, the Gates Foundation, the Economist Intelligence Unit, and WORLD Policy Analysis Center, http://noceilings. org/report/report.pdf.